Inequality, Poverty, and History

Inequality, Poverty, and History

The Kuznets Memorial Lectures
of the Economic Growth Center,
Yale University

Jeffrey G. Williamson

Basil Blackwell

Library of Congress Cataloging in Publication Data

Williamson, Jeffrey G., 1935–
  Inequality, poverty, and history: the Kuznets memorial
lectures / Jeffrey G. Williamson.
      p.   cm.
  Includes index.
  ISBN 1-55786-118-8 (hardback)
  1. Income distribution—History. 2. Poverty—History.
3. Saving and investment—History. 4. Industry—History.
I. Title.
II. Title: Kuznets memorial lectures.
HC79.I5W55 1991   90–39267
339.2'09—dc20   CIP

British Library Cataloguing in Publication Data
A CIP catalogue record for this book is available from the British
Library.

Typeset in 10½ on 12 pt Baskerville
by Photo·graphics, Honiton, Devon
Printed in Great Britain by Billing & Sons Ltd, Worcester

Contents

Preface by Series Editor

In 1986 the Economic Growth Center of Yale University established a lecture series in honor of the late Simon Kuznets, who participated in founding the Center in 1961 and served thereafter on its Executive Committee until his death in 1985. Kuznets received the Nobel Prize in Economics in 1971. This Memorial Lecture Series is dedicated to "Quantitative Aspects of the Economic Growth Among Nations," the title Simon Kuznets selected for his pioneering series of ten short monographs that were published by *The Journal of Economic Development and Cultural Change* from 1956 to 1967.

The lectures have been endowed by the generosity of gifts received from numerous friends and colleagues of Simon Kuznets from many parts of the world, as well as by a contribution from the Economic Growth Center.

The first series of lectures was presented at Yale University in March 1987 by Angus Deaton of Princeton University on "Household Behavior in Developing Countries." In April 1988 Amartya Sen of Harvard University presented the second series of Kuznets Memorial Lectures entitled "Inequality Reexamined." Included here is the third set of lectures presented in September 1989 by Jeffrey G. Williamson of Harvard University on "Inequality and Modern Economic Growth: What Does History Tell Us?"

Jeffrey Williamson, Laird Bell Professor of Economics and

Master of Mather House, is known for his many books and articles on economic history and economic development. One of his major contributions is to describe modern economic growth as it occurred during the industrial revolution in England, the United States and Japan, as well as in contemporary low-income countries, such as India. The framework that has unified much of his work is a computable general equilibrium model of the development process that assumes supply and demand equilibrate, or that prices and wages are flexible and thus clear markets. This neoclassical tradition could be contrasted with that of the Lewis-Fei-Ranis model in which wages are not flexible. A second focus of Williamson's research employs these models to explain regularities in inequality of personal incomes during the industrial revolution. His lectures analytically integrate these two themes. Williamson demonstrates why income inequality need not increase before it decreases with modern development, as Kuznets himself postulated in his 1960 presidential address to the American Economic Association. These lectures by Professor Williamson are a *tour de force* that should stimulate the thinking of any student of development or economic history.

T. Paul Schultz
Director of the Economic Growth Center
Yale University, New Haven, Connecticut

Introduction

For those of us who began our academic careers in the early 1960s, explanations of the inequality of the wealth of nations was clearly the most urgent question on the research agenda. We were certainly living in unusual times, since the growth performance of the world economy was unusually fast by historical standards. Perhaps most surprisingly, the growth performance in the Third World was also spectacular by historical standards.

The facts are that Third World per capita income growth after 1950 was more than three times that of nineteenth-century Europe. The comparison between growth then and now is, of course, an average of fast growers, slow growers, and basket cases, but the finding is confirmed if the comparison is restricted to fast-growing NICs (newly industrialized countries) who were and are catching up to the leaders. The important NICs of the nineteenth century were Germany and the United States, catching up and eventually overtaking the United Kingdom, the leader who underwent the first industrial revolution. The NICs in the Third World today can be characterized by the nine fastest growers over the quarter century 1950–75 (a group including the People's Republic of China), and their average growth was also more than three times that of Germany and the United States in the nineteenth century.

In short, we are living in an unusual period of very dramatic Third World industrial revolutions, far more dramatic than those achieved in the nineteenth century. Furthermore, what was true of the "growth miracle" between 1950 and 1975, was still true after productivity slowdown: per capita growth performance in the Third World since 1975 has been double that of the nineteenth century industrializers.

No miracles were expected in 1950. Even the experts were surprised since there was no reason to think that the Third World would do any better than the nineteenth-century industrializers. Indeed, even *that* more modest achievement was unexpected. Economists simply did not appreciate how far many of the countries in the Third World had come since 1850 in setting the preconditions to modern industrialization. Thus, the actual performance over the four decades following 1950 exceeded, by far, all expectations.

Since they did not know their history, most laymen and even many economists did not appreciate the magnitude of this achievement. We simply had not devoted much empirical attention to problems of growth prior to the 1950s. Simon Kuznets changed all that, and his impact was so great that these memorial lectures given at Yale in September 1989 have been named in his honor. Kuznets raised the big questions about modern economic growth. He started us thinking about the sources of the growth, about problems of accumulation, and about the demographic transition. He also started us thinking about who gains from growth, a topic central to the thinking of classical economists who placed inequality at the center of their models as they struggled to understand the First Industrial Revolution which was unfolding in Britain two centuries ago. Simon Kuznets also had a great appreciation for comparative history: the message of his work was clearly that we cannot understand the present without understanding the past.

In my darker moments, I sometimes feel we have lost sight of Kuznets's message. Caught up in the urgency of contemporary crises, development economists today seem to be less interested in the big questions informed by economic history than was an older generation who eagerly read Kuznets when he began publishing his articles in *Economic Development and Cultural Change* in the 1950s. Indeed, there seems to be a growing gap between contemporary development economics and economic history. What a great irony this is since we now know far more about past industrial revolutions than we did three decades ago. To put it quite bluntly, economic history is far better equipped to educate contemporary debate in the Third World than it was back in the 1950s and 1960s when Simon Kuznets was making his prodigious contributions. To plagiarize Alex Cairncross, perhaps economic historians should mount a deliberate effort of vulgarization to attract more attention and to communicate our findings. While I hope readers will not view my lectures as vulgar pamphleteering, they will focus on what economic historians have learned over the past decade or so, rather than offer new research. I will take this opportunity to repeat some of those messages, and to muse over what my collaborators and I have found.

Where shall I start? The territory Simon Kuznets staked out is much too vast to cover in the four lectures which follow (the first three of which were given at Yale, the last of which has been taken from a background paper for *The World Development Report 1990* written with Ben Polak), so I will focus on inequality, poverty, and accumulation – vast enough as it is. These were certainly the big topics in the early and mid 1970s before we got distracted by oil price shocks, productivity slowdown, and debt crises. However, there are signs that we are rediscovering inequality and poverty. These signs include Amartya Sen's work on famine and entitlements as well as the fact that the 1990 *World Development Report* will focus on the distributional impact of structural adjustment.

Before I begin, I would like to acknowledge and thank my collaborators who over the years have joined me in enriching our understanding of the industrial revolution past and present. These include most prominently Charles Becker, Timothy Hatton, Allen Kelley, Peter Lindert, Edwin Mills, and Ben Polak. They will recognize the argument and, in some cases, the language which appears in the lectures which follow. The published results of our collaborations are listed in the bibliography. They are not, of course, responsible for any errors that have crept into these lectures, but the references to our collaborations at the end of the book make it clear how much they have contributed to my thinking. I also want to acknowledge T. Paul Schultz who hosted these lectures at Yale with such grace, hospitality, and scholarly elegance, and Ariel Pakes whose comments helped me revise an earlier draft.

1

Lecture One
Inequality and the Industrial Revolution

1 Setting the Stage

Do industrial revolutions breed inequality? Opinion has always been in ready supply on this old chestnut, and the 150 years of experience with industrial revolutions since it all started in Britain has done little to diminish debate. Furthermore, opinions about the past color our view of inequality trends that we believe the Third World should anticipate today. The debate has persisted in part because the participants rarely gathered hard evidence to document inequality trends before World War One. One can sympathize, since few hard data were available then, and the distant past offers only modest clues even now. Lack of evidence, however, never squelched debate on a hot issue like this one.

After a two-year visit to England, Friedrich Engels fired the opening shot in 1845. His first major work deplored the condition of the working class in no uncertain terms, and apologists for capitalism have been on the defensive ever since. Before the industrial revolution, Engels tells us,

> The workers enjoyed a comfortable and peaceful existence . . .
> Their standard of life was much better than that of the factory
> worker today. They were not forced to work excessive hours

[and] most of them were strong, well-built people. (*quoted in Williamson, 1985a, p. 1*)

Three years later, *The Communist Manifesto* added the final touches to the classic description of middle- and lower-class impoverishment in the midst of accelerating economy-wide productivity growth:

> Those who have hitherto belonged to the lower middle class – small manufacturers, small traders, minor recipients of unearned income, handicraftsmen, and peasants – slip down, one and all, into the proletariat . . . Private property has been abolished for nine-tenths of the population; it exists only because these nine-tenths have none of it. (*quoted in Williamson, 1989a, p. 2*)

Two decades later, these opinions became a "General Law of Capitalist Accumulation" in Marx's *Das Kapital*:

> The greater the social wealth, the functioning capital, the extent and energy of its growth . . . the greater is the industrial reserve army . . . and the greater is official pauperism. *This is the absolute general law of capitalist accumulation.* (*quoted in Williamson, 1985a, p. 2*)

Like Engels, Marx asserted that the lot of the workers had grown worse, although it could be argued that both had *relative*, rather than absolute, impoverishment in mind.

Engels and Marx were hardly alone in stating publicly that inequality was on the rise in England. Speaking to the House of Commons in 1911, Philip Snowden paraphrased Marx with some parliamentary rhetoric which has since crept in to our common lexicon:

> The working people are getting poorer. The rich are getting richer . . . They are getting enormously rich. They are getting shamefully rich. They are getting dangerously rich. (*quoted in Williamson, 1985a, p. 2*)

Anyone can play the polemic game, and apologists for capitalism rose to the challenge. Porter and Giffen countered the radical critique by using limited tax return data to suggest an egalitarian trend. With equally slim evidence, Alfred Marshall added his weighty influence to the optimistic camp.

This exchange between the critics and defenders of capitalism has been going on now for at least 150 years since the British reform debates started to heat up in the 1830s. Furthermore, there is no evidence that the exchange has cooled down, since the same intensity characterizes debate over rising inequality in Latin America and elsewhere in the industrializing Third World today. The questions pestering economists then are the same ones pestering us now. Did British capitalism breed inequality? Why? Could Britain have avoided it? How?

As we have come to appreciate, the debate has generated two hypotheses, not just one. The first we have already introduced, namely, that industrialization breeds inequality. The second hypothesis asserts the reverse causality, namely that inequality fosters accumulation and thus industrialization. While my third lecture will have much more to say about this hypothesized Smithian trade-off, suffice it to say that the British classical economists thought that inequality *did* foster accumulation and more rapid industrialization. For at least a century and a half, mainstream economists and government officials were guided by the belief that the national product could not be raised if the poor were given a larger share. After all, did not redistribution from rich to poor diminish the surplus available for accumulation?

As I have already advertised, this first lecture shall focus on the first hypothesis, that industrialization breeds inequality. It draws heavily on my own work and that in collaboration with Peter Lindert.

2 The Kuznets Curve: Contemporary Cross-Sections

In his presidential address to the American Economic Association more than three decades ago, Simon Kuznets (1955) noted that income inequality seemed to have declined in the industrialized nations across the mid twentieth century, and ventured the guess that it had risen earlier just as the critics of capitalism had asserted. While Kuznets was drawing on limited historical evidence, others in the 1970s rose to his challenge by pursuing the more abundant cross-sectional evidence. Felix Paukert (1973), Irma Adelman and Cynthia Taft Morris (1978), Hollis Chenery and his World Bank team (1974), Montek Ahluwalia (1976, 1980), and Edmar Bacha (1979), all thought they saw contemporary cross-section evidence supporting the Kuznets Curve, namely that income inequality first rose and then declined with development.

The Kuznets Curve is illustrated in figure 1.1, based on Ahluwalia's World Bank sample. A quadratic fits this 60-country sample fairly well, where the inequality statistic is simply the income share of the top 20 per cent. The underlying data can and have been criticized. Indeed, some have argued that the data is much too fragile to resolve the debate. But whatever your position on the issue of data quality, two morals leap out from figure 1.1. First, the more robust portion of the Kuznets Curve lies to the right: income inequality falls with the advance of per capita income at higher levels of development. Second, the variance around the estimated Kuznets Curve is greatest from low to middle levels of development. This second point is often forgotten by those who accept such evidence, and it has important implications: inequality is unlikely to rise systematically across a pooled cross-section of early industrial revolutions; even if most countries undergo increasing inequality during early modern economic growth, such correlations are bound to be poor since history has given less developed countries very different starting points; and some countries may avoid increasing inequality during early modern economic growth precisely because history has given them different starting points.

Let me expand on this point a bit. Production in traditional agrarian economies tends to be driven by two inputs, land and unskilled labor. In some traditional agrarian economies, like the European old world and the Latin American new

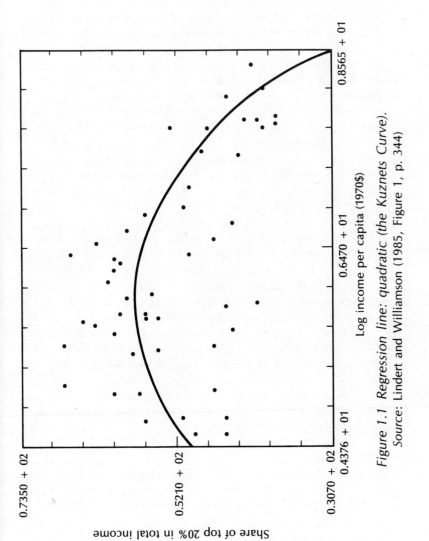

Figure 1.1 Regression line: quadratic (the Kuznets Curve).
Source: Lindert and Williamson (1985, Figure 1, p. 344)

world, the holdings of the asset which matters, land, was highly concentrated, much more highly concentrated than was human or physical capital in urban sectors. The forces of inequality driven by industrialization must push hard to increase aggregate inequality in such economies as the sector where assets and incomes are most unequally distributed declines in relative importance. Such economies will have higher inequality in early stages of development, but they may exhibit less steep upswings on the Kuznets Curve. By contrast, other traditional agrarian economies, like East Asia, Africa, and the American North, had less concentrated land holdings and more equal agrarian income distributions. Such economies are likely to exhibit lower inequality in early stages of development, but they may exhibit more steep upswings on the Kuznets Curve, *ceteris paribus*. The *ceteris paribus* is important, since the initial Latin inequality may create a path-dependent inegalitarian regime throughout the Latin industrial revolution, just as the initial East Asian equality may create a path-dependent egalitarian regime throughout the East Asian industrial revolution. These issues of initial conditions and path dependence are important, and we will take them up again in Lecture Three.

It's hard to say much more about figure 1.1. The literature doesn't tell us an awful lot about why a Kuznets Curve should appear in the first place. The data do not tell us anything about the dynamic which produces the Kuznets Curve in such cross-section data, nor why some countries are likely to depart from the curve. It turns out that history helps out on both counts.

3 The Kuznets Curve: Inequality Histories

Were Today's Industrialized Countries Always Egalitarian?

Figure 1.1 documents that the industrialized countries of today, to the far right on the diagram, are far more egalitarian than most NICs of today – bunched in the middle of the diagram. Were they always so egalitarian? They were not. In fact, inequality in Europe and America was at its zenith on the eve of World War One, and the extent of that inequality was very similar to the most inegalitarian NICs of today, like Brazil.

The quality of the available data around the turn of the century makes international inequality comparisons hazardous. Yet a rough comparison can be offered since the early years of this century were ones for which several countries reported information of a similar kind – the distribution of income based on taxes as well as the distribution of wealth based on probates. What does this evidence suggest? In the late nineteenth century, inequality was very high by almost any standard, and it was highest in Britain. It is difficult today to find any developing country where the top 5 per cent receive almost 50 per cent of the income or where the top 1 per cent hold 70 per cent of the wealth. Perhaps only such "bad Latins" as contemporary Peru, Panama, and Brazil can claim that dubious distinction. Figure 1.2 shows much the same. Here we plot two contemporary NICs: Korea – a "virtuous Asian" with a fairly egalitarian distribution; and Brazil – a "bad Latin" with a very inegalitarian distribution. Four European NICs around World War One – the United Kingdom (1913), Prussia (1913), Denmark (1908), and the Netherlands (1919) – all tend to fall in between these bounds, but they look much more like Brazil in the upper ranges in the size distribution. In short, today's industrialized countries had inequality levels on the eve of World War One similar to the most inegalitarian of today's NICS.

The Downside of the Kuznets Curve and Twentieth-century Inequality Histories

Europe and America were not always so egalitarian, it seems. So, when did the egalitarian leveling take place? We have far better evidence to answer that question today than Kuznets had in 1955.

What Arthur Burns saw in America as a "revolutionary leveling" after 1929 apparently was shared by most of Europe, whose experience is documented in figure 1.3. What is so

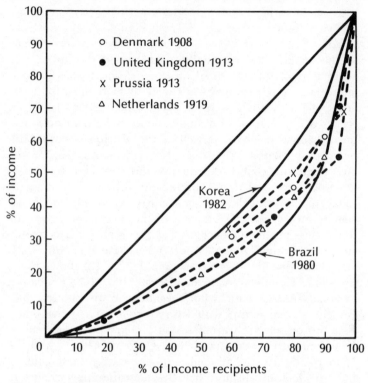

Figure 1.2 Income inequality among the NICs then and now: contemporary Korea and Brazil compared with four European nations around World War One.
Source: Polak and Williamson (1989, Figure 2)

striking about figure 1.3 is the extraordinary similarity in each national downswing of the Kuznets Curve across the twentieth century. The one possible exception is Germany in the interwar decades, but still the conformity is striking. Nor is the historical pattern in figure 1.3 unique. When these twentieth-century time series are pooled with the contemporary cross-section in figure 1.1, neither the levels nor the trends show significantly different patterns than those already summarized in figure 1.1. Thus, twentieth-century history agrees with the international cross-sections and with Kuznets's original conjecture: there is a clear trend towards equality in the later stages of development.

A Word About Market Forces Versus the Fisc

The inequality we have been talking about thus far is pre-fisc, that is, income before the effects of taxes, transfers, or government purchases of goods and services. There are three reasons for the choice. First, and certainly most pragmatic, comparative assessments are far easier to make since the literature is dominated by pre-fisc estimates. Second, while well-being at any point in time is certainly better gauged by post-fisc income, it is not at all clear that inequality trends can be explained by changes in the "fisc." Indeed, there is considerable evidence, recently reviewed by Peter Lindert (1989), that fiscal redistribution explains only a small part of the leveling in post-fisc incomes among the industrialized countries across the twentieth century. The same is true of today's international cross-sections: the contrast in post-fisc gini coefficients between egalitarian Britain and inegalitarian Brazil owes much less to fiscal redistribution and far more to pre-fisc inequalities as they are generated in the marketplace. Third, the economist is presented with a greater challenge in explaining pre-fisc inequality since it is the complex outcome of a whole range of macroeconomic forces which influence factor rewards, forces which the economist is better equipped to analyze. Even so, a case can be made that the same market forces which produced the pre-fisc leveling of incomes in industrialized countries across the twentieth century also produced a more activist government fiscal intervention, serving only to reinforce the egalitarian trends set in motion by market forces. In short, pre-fisc market forces have been at the heart of twentieth-century egalitarian trends among the industrialized countries.

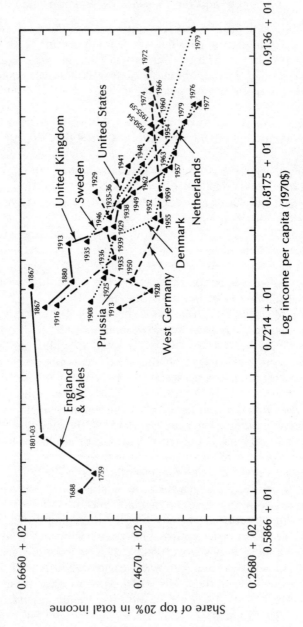

Figure 1.3 The Kuznets Curve: mostly the twentieth-century downswing.
Source: Lindert and Williamson (1985, Figure 2, p. 345)

The Upswing of the Kuznets Curve and Nineteenth-century Inequality Histories

It appears that we can document a twentieth-century egalitarian leveling for a large number of currently industrialized countries. Did they also undergo a rise in inequality when industrializing in the nineteenth century, thus confirming the Kuznets hypothesis? Here the evidence is thinner, but at least we have detailed evidence on two countries that matter, Britain in the old world, and America in the new world. Let's start with Britain and the First Industrial Revolution.

While the evidence is *still* being hotly debated, what we do have suggests that British capitalism did breed inequality, and the inequality drift seems to have been a product of the forces associated with the industrial revolution. The rise in inequality can be dated from around 1760, and it was manifested throughout the full income distribution: the income shares at the top rose, the shares at the bottom fell, real wages of the unskilled were relatively stable, the premium on skills increased, and the earnings distribution widened. The French wars interrupted the process, but the rise in inequality picked up following 1815. British inequality seems to have reached a peak somewhere around the 1860s or shortly thereafter. While not spectacular, the egalitarian leveling up to World War One was universal: as figure 1.3 suggests, the income shares at the top fell; in addition, the shares at the bottom rose, the relative pay of the unskilled improved, the premium on skills declined, and the earnings distribution narrowed. A sample of the data which supports this interpretation can be found in table 1.1.

Given that the debate over capitalism and inequality has been so intense since Marx and Engels fired their first shots, it seems unlikely that all participants will ever be satisfied with the evidence, or that all the evidence will unambiguously confirm the Kuznets Curve. And so it comes as no surprise that Charles Feinstein (1988) believes that the evidence exaggerates the rise in British inequality up to the 1860s, and that while Peter Lindert (1986) finds plenty of evidence of increasing wealth concentration in the eighteenth century, he finds little

Table 1.1 Conjectures on British Income Inequality Trends, 1688–1913

Date of original observation	Gini coefficient	Bottom 40%	Income Shares (%) 40-65% group	65-90% group	Top 10%	Top 5%	Atkinson Index $\epsilon = 1.5$	$\epsilon = 2.5$	$\epsilon = 4.0$
England and Wales									
1688	0.468	15.4	16.7	26.0	42.0	27.6	0.393	0.491	0.569
1759	0.487	15.8	14.1	25.8	44.4	31.2	0.399	0.474	0.531
1801/3	0.519	13.4	13.3	28.0	45.4	29.8	0.450	0.542	0.607
1867	0.551	14.8	11.7	20.8	52.7	45.1	0.473	0.523	0.562
United Kingdom									
1867	0.538	15.2		32.4	52.4	46.8	0.464	0.510	0.547
1880	0.520	17.0		28.8	54.2	49.4	0.462	0.502	0.532
1913	0.502	17.2		33.0	49.8	43.8	0.427	0.475	0.522

Source: Williamson (1985a, Table 4.5, p. 68)

for the nineteenth century. But the evidence supporting the British Kuznets Curve seems strong enough to warrant serious attention to the causes of the Kuznets Curve.

Before leaving the evidence, one important finding must be stressed. Most of the changes in British inequality across the nineteenth century seem to have been driven by changes in factor rewards – the structure of pay by skill, rents on land relative to wages of labor, and the returns to capital relative to other inputs – and much less by changes in the distribution of factor ownership. Changes in earnings inequality are explained primarily by changes in the structure of pay rather than by employment shifts from occupations with low skill content to those with high. While skills may well have become more equally distributed in the late nineteenth century, it was the erosion in the premium on those skills, and the relative increase in unskilled labor scarcity, that did most of the work in narrowing the earnings distribution after the 1860s. Similarly, the increase in the top 5 percent's share in national income across the French Wars had little to do with increased concentration of landed wealth – although such increases may well have taken place – but rather with the behavior of rents themselves. Changes in the distribution of wealth induced by accumulation served to reinforce the influence of changes in factor rewards on the distribution of income, but it was initial changes in factor rewards that seemed to matter in setting the Kuznets Curve in motion, and contributing to turning points. This is an important moral to remember when we start to search for explanations of the British Kuznets Curve.

So much for the old world. What about the new? Did America avoid the rising inequality which appears to have beset Britain? Apparently not. Income and wealth inequality rose sharply with the onset of modern economic growth early in the nineteenth century. Egalitarian trends only appear with the advent of mature capitalist development in the twentieth century. In the interim, America generated seven decades of pronounced inequality not unlike that experienced by Britain, or, as we have seen, by contemporary Brazil. Thus, in spite of abundant land, alleged equality of opportunity, democratic institutions, and a nineteenth-century reputation as an ideal poor man's country, America did not avoid the economic inequality commonly believed by some to be associated with capitalist development (Williamson and Lindert, 1980). Table 1.2 offers a sample of the kind of evidence which supports this conclusion, where benchmark estimates of wealth concentration are summarized over the past two centuries. Other evidence on income and earnings reinforces those trends, and fills in some of the details, but, like Britain, it is not without its critics (Margo and Villaflor, 1987).

In short, there seems to be sufficient evidence to at least tentatively confirm Kuznets's hypothesis for Britain and America. Debate over the numbers underlying these two inequality histories, as well as those underlying the contem-

Table 1.2 Wealth Inequality in the United States, 1774–1962

	Share held by Top 1%	*Share held by Top 10%*	*Gini Coefficient*
1774			
Free households	12.6%	49.6%	0.642
All households	14.8	55.1	n.a.
Free adult males	12.4	48.7	0.632
All adult males	13.2	54.3	n.a.
1860			
Free adult males	29.0	73.0	0.832
Adult males	30.3–35.0	74.6–79.0	n.a.
1870			
Adult males	27.0	70.0	0.833
1962			
All consumer units	15.1	35.7	n.a.

Source: Williamson and Lindert (1980, Table 3.1, pp. 38–9)

porary cross-section in figure 1.1, will, no doubt, continue, but surely it is time to respond to Kuznets's challenge by offering explanations of the Kuznets Curve. Surely it is time to ask why some countries were likely to undergo sharply rising inequality during their industrial revolutions while others were not, and why all of them seem to have undergone a leveling in late stages of development.

4 Theorizing about the Kuznets Curve

Focus on Factor Markets

Can inequality trends be explained without reference to changes in factor returns? Were this possible, then the nasty complexity of modeling the entire macroeconomic structure of factor returns could be avoided. Unfortunately, most of the observed movements in measured inequality appear to stem from changes in the relative rates of factor returns, so the macro-modeling cannot be avoided. Classical economists knew this well enough so that their dynamic models of growth and distribution focused on factor incomes accruing to labor, land, and capital. Modern human capital theory implies the same, with focus on the structure of pay by skill.

Kuznets himself wondered if his curve might not be the result of shifts in employment alone, and Sherman Robinson (1976) gave the idea some empirical plausibility. Stripped to its essentials, the argument goes something like this. Imagine a society characterized by perfect equality, with everyone earning 5 pesos. Let some modernizing influence introduce a job paid at 10 pesos, which is first enjoyed by just one lucky individual and then diffuses through society until everyone earns the 10 pesos. Any conventional inequality measure will rise from the initial perfect equality and then return to it later, tracing out the Kuznets Curve.

While simple and elegant, there are limits to any inequality explanation which relies solely on this kind of job diffusion process. It is not true that inequality histories are driven solely or even primarily by such forces. Pay advantages themselves have a tendency to rise and fall as we have seen in the British and American cases. Indeed, over half the observed rise in aggregate earnings inequality in nineteenth-century Britain stemmed from movements in these pay ratios by skill. Symmetrically, the collapse of pay ratios accounted for more than half of the drop in American earnings inequality following 1939.

The pattern of rising and falling pay ratios is sufficiently widespread, and so closely parallels overall inequality trends, that it suggests that any theory of the Kuznets Curve must explain why rates of pay first diverge and then converge during modern economic growth.

What about the distribution of non-human wealth? In principle, one might imagine that changes in the distribution of wealth might be an independent determinant of changes in income inequality. Although changes in wealth distributed associated with slave emancipation, land reform, civil war, and nationalization may be loosely associated with the stresses of modern economic growth, and while they may help account for idiosyncratic experience in some national histories, they cannot offer any coherent explanation of the Kuznets Curve. It seems more appropriate to view long-run trends in the distribution of wealth either as a result of previous changes in the distribution of income or as a simultaneous outcome, since those forces driving returns to assets surely also govern the aggregate value and distribution of wealth.

We are led, then, back to factor markets in searching for the sources of inequality, and to labor markets in particular. So it is that economic historians and development economists have pondered at length how labor markets work in economies shocked by the disequilibrium of industrial revolutions and demographic transitions. And so it is that Jan Tinbergen (1975) has focused on a model of labor markets to account for the twentieth-century leveling of income and earnings in the industrialized economies. What follows is in that tradition: I look for the microeconomic foundations of what appears to be a macroeconomic event – the Kuznets Curve. Furthermore, as we try to uncover the factor-demand and factor-supply forces that drive inequality, the explanation should also be consistent with the pattern and rate of economic growth. Growth and distribution require a simultaneous attack whether we believe in the Smithian trade-off or not – another old chestnut awaiting us in Lecture Three. So, how might factor demand and supply forces have operated in the past to produce the Kuznets Curve?

Labor-Saving Technological Change

A potentially powerful factor-demand force behind the distribution of income is the degree to which technological progress tends to economize on some factors of production while favoring the use of others. A bias toward unskilled-labor saving can widen income gaps by worsening job prospects and wages for the unskilled while bidding up the returns to skills, capital, and perhaps even land. This idea is hardly novel, but the evidence on long-run, systematic movements in the factor demand bias needs to be established, as well as its correlation with the Kuznets Curve. We *do* know that American growth in the nineteenth century was heavily unskilled labor saving, and the same seems to have been true of Britain prior to 1860. Most would argue that the same has been true of the Third World since 1950. But is there any evidence suggesting that these high rates of unskilled-labor saving abate as nations approach maturity? Third World experience is, of course, too short to offer any guidance, but Britain's experience with productivity slowdown around the turn of the century appears to be consistent with sharp retardation, if not reversal, in the rate of unskilled-labor saving. But America offers the most comprehensive evidence by far. For the economy as a whole, each of several studies has found a strong aggregate labor-saving bias from about the start of this century to 1929, followed by a switch to either neutrality or a labor-using bias up to the Korean War. None of these studies actually distinguished between unskilled and skilled labor, but it may be surmised that any era of labor saving was likely to have been especially unskilled labor saving. Thus, the downswing of the Kuznets Curve which starts in the late nineteenth century in Britain and after 1929 in America may have been due to a switch in the bias of aggregate technological progress from unskilled labor saving which preceded those dates.

It is important at this point to pause and remind ourselves what we mean by aggregate labor saving. Aggregate labor saving can appear in the historical data for any of the following four reasons:

1 labor saving – including what has come to be called de-skilling – induced by a rise in labor's relative scarcity;
2 shifts in industrial output mix away from labor-intensive sectors induced by shifts in product demand or factor supply forces;
3 differences in the rate of technological advance between industries of different labor intensities; and
4 the introduction of labor-saving technologies within industries.

Two of these can be dismissed right at the start. The first source of labor saving is not a source at all, but rather only a response to relative labor scarcities. The last – labor saving at the industry level – was a favorite econometric exercise a decade or two ago, but nothing in that literature establishes any historical pattern, Kuznetsian or otherwise. The second and third sources appear to be more promising. Let me expand on each.

It is certainly true that one of the stylized facts of development is the shift in output and employment mix as economies undergo the transition from an agrarian base to advanced industrialization. Thus, the rate at which agriculture declines as a share of aggregate output or employment begins slowly, then quickens, reaching a peak as the industrial revolution hits full stride, and then drops off as the transformation is completed at late stages of development. To the extent that agriculture is relatively unskilled labor intensive, high and rising aggregate unskilled labor saving early in the industrial revolution should be followed by a fall in the rate of aggregate unskilled labor saving late in the development process. If these derived labor demand forces are strong enough, the Kuznets Curve is assured.

Convenient and elegant, this explanation does not go far enough. Unbalanced output growth such as this cannot be viewed as an exogenous force driving inequality across the Kuznets Curve if endogenous domestic demand forces – like Engel Effects – account for it. How much of the spectacular shift in output mix in the Third World today or in Britain and America in the last century can be explained by the rapid rate of technological progress outside of unskilled labor intensive agriculture? How much of the shift can be explained by trade and domestic policies of "urban bias" which favor capital/skill-intensive activities, and how much by favorable world market conditions in those sectors? How much of it is due to changes in the structure of demand, as households respond to higher incomes? The key point here is simply that the sectoral shift itself is not an independent influence on inequality unless it can be shown that it comes from exogenous forces, like policies, world markets, and what I call unbalanced productivity advance. Further, we then have to show that these exogenous forces are themselves correlated with the Kuznets Curve. One of these with some promise is the urban bias, a topic of Lecture Two. A second is unbalanced productivity advance.

An extensive literature has sketched the sectoral patterns of total factor productivity growth over the last 150 years in America. The secular movements do indeed trace out a nineteenth-century drift away from labor-using sectors, largely because productivity advance was rapid in capital and skill-intensive manufacturing and transportation, while large and labor-intensive agriculture lagged far behind. Early in this century the same labor-saving imbalance between sectors continued up to World War One and across the 1920s. Between 1929 and 1953, the sectoral pattern was much more balanced, with agriculture in particular catching up with the rest of the economy. To summarize, the rise and fall in the rate of labor saving associated with unbalanced productivity advance seems to correlate well with the American Kuznets Curve.

Although not as well documented, a similar pattern seems to have characterized British experience. Between 1780 and 1860, technological progress was very unbalanced in favor of the capital/skills-intensive sectors, shifting factor demand away from unskilled labor. After 1860, the sectoral pattern of British productivity advance was far more balanced in its factor-demand effects. Like twentieth-century America, late nineteenth-century Britain's farm sector switched from a large, unskilled labor intensive activity with relatively slow productivity advance to a small sector with average capital intensity and productivity performance. And once again, the timing of the switch to more balanced productivity advance coincided with a historic peak in the Kuznets Curve.

"Classic" patterns of unbalanced productivity advance like those revealed by American and British history hold promise in helping account for the Kuznets Curve when it appears. As long as product demands are elastic – as in the open economy case, then rapid productivity advance off the farm will pull resources from agriculture. Since traditional agriculture uses unskilled labor in large doses and since modern urban activities use unskilled labor in smaller doses, the demand for unskilled labor softens relative to capital and skills, unskilled wages lag behind, the bottom of the income distribution suffers, and history traces out the upswing of the Kuznets Curve. American and British history also suggest that evidence of the Kuznets Curve is likely to be most striking for those countries whose technological history has been most unbalanced, and for whom agriculture has lagged most behind, *ceteris paribus*. The Kuznets Curve is most likely to be absent in those countries who have been most successful in avoiding unbalanced productivity advance. One such example seems to be Japan. There is no clear drift in the rate of labor saving implied by the intersectoral pattern of Japanese productivity advance from the 1880s to the 1930s. Japan also seems to have avoided the Kuznets Curve over the past century.

Immigration, Demographic Transitions, and Labor Supplies

It has become commonplace in the historical literature to associate the demographic transition with labor surplus and inequality. The argument develops along the following lines: modern economic growth begins on a traditional agrarian base characterized by elastic labor supplies, better known as surplus unskilled labor. Accelerating rates of capital accumulation associated with early industrialization thus fail to generate rising wages among the unskilled until the surplus labor pool is exhausted. This turning point can be postponed for some time if demographic forces are right and Malthusian pressures or immigration continually replenish the initial pool. Under such conditions stable real wages for the unskilled could coincide with rising per capita incomes, tending to create more inequality.

Remember that this classical model of capitalist growth was built by British economists surrounded by the poverty and pauperism of early nineteenth-century Britain which appears to have been on the upswing of the Kuznets Curve. Although the mid-twentieth century version of the classical model certainly had its critics, it quickly became the dominant paradigm used by Third World observers to analyze exactly the same set of problems which attracted the British classical economists. The application of the model to Britain was encouraged in part by the forces of demographic transition there – primarily increases in fertility, but also by improvements in infant mortality and by Irish immigration into Britain's industrial north.

Increased fertility and immigration associated with the industrial revolution should foster income inequality in two ways. First, it gluts labor markets with young and unskilled new entrants, creating massive changes in the age distribution of the population and the labor force. Such changes in the age distribution can create inequality even if factor prices and the structure of incomes are unaffected, as Simon Kuznets (1976), Samuel Morley (1981), and others have noted. That is, there will be more at the bottom of the distribution than before. Second, the glut lowers the relative wage of unskilled labor, while raising the returns to skills and conventional capital, thus fostering inequality. It also follows that those countries which have been beset with external immigrations during their industrial revolutions are more likely to exhibit rising inequality and the upswing of the Kuznets Curve (like the new world). Similarly, those countries which underwent significant external emigration during their industrial revolutions are more likely to have avoided rising inequality (like the old world). In addition, those countries which underwent more dramatic demographic transitions are far more likely to trace out unambiguous Kuznets Curves in their historical data than those who did not (like France and Japan).

The American immigration–inequality literature has relied largely on raw correlations between inequality and the labor supply. The correlations are not hard to document. For example, the period of highest labor force growth, from 1820 to 1860, was also one of rising skill premiums, wage stretching, and wage inequality, while the period of lowest labor force growth, 1929–48, ·was one of dramatic leveling in earnings and incomes. The intervening observations reveal a fairly tight positive correlation as well. In terms of immigrations, new arrivals from abroad – who tended to be relatively unskilled – had their biggest impact on the growth of the American labor force in the 15 years prior to the Civil War, and between the 1890s and World War One. These were also periods of especially sharp increases in inequality along the upswing of the American Kuznets Curve. After the mid 1920s and the imposition of the quotas, the immigrant flows became a much lower share of the domestic labor force, presumably contributing to the downswing of the American Kuznets Curve. Presumably, the downside of the Kuznets Curve shared by so many advanced economies in the twentieth century is in part due to shared experience with forces of population slowdown generated by common experience with the demographic transition.

Human Capital Accumulation and Skills Deepening

As early as 1848, John Stuart Mill predicted that an acceleration in skills acquisition would eventually erase the skills scarcity and resulting earnings inequality generated by the industrial revolution. That proposition has remained untested for more than a century, and it is clearly relevant to understanding the Kuznets Curve. After all, it wasn't until the 1960s that Gary Becker and Theodore Schultz started us quantifying human capital formation. Since then, there has been a veritable flood of empirical work documenting labor force quality trends, including some recent estimates for both nineteenth-century America and Britain.

These estimates suggest that the rate of skills deepening (that is, the rise in skills per member of the labor force) correlates well (and inversely) with skills scarcity, earnings inequality, and income inequality. The rate of skills deepening was exceedingly low in Britain during her early phase of rising wage inequality; the pace quickened around mid century, about a decade after Mill's observation; and the rate of skills deepening reached impressive levels in the era following the educational reforms of the 1870s, coinciding with the first drop down Britain's Kuznets Curve. The American correlation looks similar, though the turning points come later, well into the twentieth century, both for the rate of skills deepening and for the leveling of incomes. The historical evidence from these two countries at least suggests a slow equilibrating process, whereby one generation's skilled-wage gap promotes the next generation's faster accumulation of skills. The institutional and economic arrangements which make the human capital accumulation response rapid in some countries (like East Asia) and slower in others (like Latin America) clearly will play a role in determining whether a Kuznets Curve will be more pronounced in some countries compared with others.

What About Capital Accumulation?

So far, we haven't said a word about capital accumulation. The reason is that the influence is more complex, although we used to think it was straightforward. Back in simpler days when we thought in terms of capital and labor only, and given that the elasticity of substitution between the two was less than one, then it followed that accumulation raised labor's share and diminished inequality. Reality is more complex, especially when we think in terms of three factors – labor, skills, and capital – and when we also worry about the source of capital accumulation.

If our interest were confined to the earnings distribution and the skilled-wage ratio, it would be a simple matter to predict the effects of capital accumulation. History tells us that capital tends to be complementary with skills and a substitute for unskilled labor, so a rise in the capital stock should augment the skilled-wage ratio and earnings inequality. Furthermore, an increase in the capital stock implies an increase in the relative size of the capital goods sector, the more so are capital goods produced at home. History tells us that the capital goods sector tends to use skilled labor intensively, so the demand for skills is driven up and we have another force tending to raise the skilled-wage ratio and earnings inequality.

The impact of capital accumulation on inequality becomes more difficult to identify when our interest shifts from earnings inequality to income inequality. Suppose an outward shift in the supply of savings – due to a rise in domestic thrift or to an inflow of foreign investment – creates capital deepening. The augmented supply of capital will raise the skilled-wage ratio and earnings inequality for the reasons already offered, but it is also likely to lower the return to capital. Since capital's return is diminished while earnings inequality is augmented, the impact on overall income inequality is ambiguous. Suppose instead that the source of the capital deepening is an improvement in capital goods supply, driven by unbalanced productivity improvements favoring the capital goods sector, and revealed by a decline in the relative price of capital goods. In this case, income inequality is clearly increased. Not only should wage stretching and increased earnings inequality take place, but the rate of return to capital should also rise as should capital's share. Finally, suppose it is some world price shock or some technological event which raises the relative demand for capital. Once again, income inequality is assured.

Obviously, the impact of capital accumulation on inequality is complex, and it may vary from country to country. If it is driven by a secular boom in investment demand or by an exogenous decline in the relative price of investment goods, inequality is assured. If instead it is driven by an exogenous rise in domestic savings or foreign capital inflows, it is *not* assured. This distinction – a topic of Lecture Three – may offer yet another reason why some countries conform to the Kuznets Curve while others do not.

So, we have three or four plausible forces that might account for the presence (or the absence) of the Kuznets Curve: labor-saving technological change – a force that Marx favored; labor supply – a force which Malthus favored; human capital accumulation – a force which Mill favored; and conventional capital accumulation – although this can hardly be viewed as an independent force if it is being driven by the first two. Plausibility is one thing, however. Fact is another. How are we to discriminate between these plausible explanations? History has a nasty way of generating multicollinearity: industrial revolutions are associated with increased labor saving, quickening rates of labor-force growth, rising accumulation rates, and anti-agrarian policies. How do you sort one out from the other?

5 What Explains the Kuznets Curve? Lessons from History

My view of inequality history, particularly in Britain and America, leads me to concentrate on fundamental trends in

factor demands and supplies associated with the industrial
revolution. To quantify these influences, I favor the use of
computable general equilibrium (CGE) models. A multisector
and multifactor CGE is especially useful for analysis of the
long run, where neoclassical assumptions do least damage to
the macroeconomic facts, and where the determinants of output mix, input use, and factor incomes are the prime focus.
   When these CGEs are applied to American and British
inequality history, what do we find?

American Experience

The surge in inequality before the Civil War seems to have
been due primarily to the extraordinary rates of capital
accumulation obtained during those decades, rates that were
generated by a secular boom in investment demand itself
pushed by rapid rates of labor-saving technological advance.
Rapid accumulation favored skilled workers towards the
middle of the distribution and capitalists towards the top of
the distribution in two ways. First, a greater proportion of
unskilled labor (a substitute for capital) than skilled labor (a
complement to capital) was replaced by mechanization.
Second, accumulation helped raise income per capita, and
this rise, through Engel's Law, caused agriculture to contract
as a share in national income, a process that released relatively
large doses of unskilled labor. Unbalanced technological progress centered on manufacturing and transport favored the
expansion of capital and skill-intensive sectors, contributing
to the rise in inequality on two counts: directly by favoring
the modern sectors where unskilled labor was used the least,
and indirectly by inducing an accumulation response with
the results already described.
   After the Civil War and as the late nineteenth century
progressed, capital accumulation became a little less rapid,
and productivity growth a bit less unbalanced. These changes
explain about half of the observed shift from sharply rising
inequality on the upswing of the Kuznets Curve, to relative
stability in those inequality trends along the Kuznets Curve's
high American plateau. Demographic events explain much of

the remainder. Skills per man hour appear to have grown significantly in the late nineteenth century after having remained stable for much of the ante-bellum period – in part due to the earlier rise in foreign immigration rates. The apparent cause of this acceleration in skills deepening and skills widening was the decline in the share of the labor force consisting of new, unskilled immigrants. The resulting rise in the rate of skills deepening helped prevent a continuation of the surge in earnings and income inequality started earlier in the century.

The first decade of the twentieth century brought a resumption of wage stretching, and rising earnings and income inequality. This time, however, the rising trend owed nothing to capital accumulation or to demographic forces. Rather, the explanation for the return to widening gaps seems to rest on a resumption of more unbalanced rates of technological progress.

Across the 1910s and 1920s, American inequality first compressed during the war and then bounced right back in the immediate post-war period, leaving no net change. There are two interesting attributes of this net stability. First, sectoral capital intensities converged. As a result, rapid accumulation after 1909 came to imply accumulation of a factor widely spread across all sectors rather than one concentrated in relatively skill-intensive sectors. It turns out that this "convergence-in-factor-intensity" helps us understand much about US twentieth-century experience with structural change. Second, if the only kind of growth from 1909 to 1929 had been growth in factor supplies, the era of income leveling would have been ushered in two decades earlier. This follows since immigration and fertility were making much smaller contributions to labor force growth, especially during World War One and after the immigration restrictions took effect in the mid 1920s. The slower labor force growth and the faster rate of skills deepening served to compress the pay structure and level earnings distributions. But in fact there was no net compression in the pay structure. Why? Because technological progress was again very unbalanced, and it centered on sectors which used a lot of skills, some capital, but little unskilled labor.

When the downswing of the American Kuznets Curve finally arrived following 1929, it was the result of the coincidence of technological and demographic forces. Total factor productivity growth was more evenly balanced across sectors than in any other era since 1840, accelerating in agriculture and some services. This change accounted for about half of the leveling between 1929 and the Korean War. Most of the remainder is explained by demographic forces: by the great fertility decline and by shutting out immigrants from the old world. The rise in government expenditures seems to have made only a very modest contribution.

As Alan Blinder (1980) and others have pointed out, the pre-fisc income distribution remained remarkably stable from Korean War to the Reagan era. Why did the twentieth-century revolutionary leveling stop? Mostly it appears to be attributable to a resumption of those demographic forces which served to raise inequality in America over the century after 1830. The sources will be well-known to many readers: the rise in married women in the labor force tended to glut the market in relatively low-wage jobs; and the baby boom cohort served to do the same. While the combined effects of a post-war influx of wives and baby boomers served to stop the leveling in incomes, they were not of the same magnitude as the earlier surges in immigration from southern and eastern Europe, so at least there was no induced rise in inequality.

British Nineteenth-century Experience

One can view the increasing inequality that appears often to accompany early industrialization as a manifestation of disequilibrium which many capitalist countries pass through as they emerge from a backward agrarian past. While inequality has been documented for many Third World economies as they experienced their industrial revolutions in the post-war period, we were never really sure about nineteenth-century capitalist development, in spite of the allegations by classical economists and the hot debate among contemporaries of that time. Nor were we really sure how much of the alleged early inequality experience might have been purely demographic, associated with the demographic transition. It now appears that America and Britain both experienced the Kuznets Curve of first rising, then falling, inequality. Nonetheless, the timing of the Kuznets Curve differed. As we have seen, British inequality seems to have peaked in the mid to late nineteenth century while American inequality remained at a plateau from the Civil War to the 1920s before starting its downswing. Why does the leveling start a half-century sooner in Britain? In any case, were the forces driving the British Kuznets Curve across the nineteenth century quantitatively similar to those which we have already documented for America? It seems so.

As with America, changes in the rate of unbalanced productivity advance and changes in the rate of skills deepening are two critical forces driving the British Kuznets Curve across the nineteenth century. The pay gaps and earnings inequality set in motion by unbalanced productivity advance – favoring relatively rapid expansion in the derived demand for skills, served to offer great and increasing incentive to investment in human capital much like John Stuart Mill alleged in 1848. However, the slow and inelastic supply response in skills per worker – explained in part by income constraints facing the poor unskilled and in part by the modest intervention by the state, both of which limited the ability of the poor to invest in human capital – made it possible for inequality to persist for many decades before the demand-side disequilibrium began to be rectified in the late nineteenth century and earnings inequality began to settle down.

One of the reasons why Britain underwent a leveling on the downside of the Kuznets Curve before America did appear to be because Britain suffered a late nineteenth-century and early twentieth-century productivity slowdown while America did not. A second explanation can be found on the factor–supply side: Britain never had to absorb increasing unskilled labor supplies from abroad after about 1850 and the Irish famines, so that she could accelerate the rate of skills deepening earlier than could America.

What About the Expenditure Side?

While the incomes of the poor lagged behind on the upswing of the Kuznets Curve in Britain and America, they also suffered on the expenditure side since the items they consumed rose sharply in relative price. That is, the same forces that caused the wages of the poor to lag behind also tended to raise the poor's living costs – industrialization in the nineteenth century cheapened the goods that the poor produced relative to the goods that the poor consumed. Unbalanced productivity advance, inelastic land supplies, and an anti-poor regime of state intervention were the critical forces that generated that result. The relative price of food and rents are crucial to the story since both loomed so large in the budgets of the poor, especially the urban poor. Both increased during periods of rising income inequality. Technological advance was fast in industry, while slow in agriculture and urban housing, thus increasing the relative price of the two wage goods most important to the poor. These technological forces were reinforced by inelastic land supplies which were, of course, more important inputs to agriculture and urban housing.

6 A Summing Up

No unambiguous theory of the Kuznets Curve emerges from this look at history. After all, no inevitable law of economic motion has emerged from history either. First, the evidence which documents inequality among industrializing nations then and now is sufficiently fragile to ensure that the debate started by Marx and Engels early in the last century will continue well into the next. Second, there is more than one path to development. Representing the old world and the new, Britain and America both seem to have satisfied the economic and demographic conditions which can generate a Kuznets Curve. These were: a rise and fall in labor saving technological change, the source of which was a rise and fall in what I have called unbalanced productivity advance centered on gaps between industry and agriculture; a rise and fall in the rate of labor force growth, the source of which was the demographic transition and foreign immigration; a very long lag in the rate of skills or human capital deepening; and a rise and fall in the rate of accumulation induced by the other forces. Not all countries satisfied these conditions: Japan, for example, seems to have missed most of the first three and thus seems to have missed the Kuznets Curve as well. What we need are more comparative nineteenth- and twentieth-century economic histories so that we can understand better the inequality impact of different paths to development and why countries choose them.

2

Lecture Two
Migration: Escaping from Rural Poverty

1 Poverty and Rural Emigration: The Conventional Wisdom

The demise of agriculture and the rise of industry was central to the historical account of the Kuznets Curve in Lecture One. There were four parts to the story, but unbalanced productivity advance favoring industry at agriculture's expense was one of the most important of the four. To make it simple, the argument was that in response to these productivity events agriculture released much heavier doses of unskilled labor than was absorbed by industry, thus diminishing the demand for unskilled labor relative to skills and capital. Rising inequality was the likely outcome. The story was in the tradition of the Kuznets Curve, a story about relative rather than absolute incomes. The present lecture shifts attention to absolutes – that is, to numbers in poverty and the real earnings of the working poor. However, the shift in the center of gravity from agriculture to industry will still occupy center stage, and rural emigration will carry it.

Let me begin with the conventional wisdom as I see it. Rural emigration can reduce poverty for three reasons: first, it involves migration to better jobs, a gain in the migrant's human condition insured by the evidence of big wage gaps between city and countryside; second, it involves migration to a labor market which offers more effective life-cycle occupational "ladders" for the migrant and his children (that is, it offers better access to modes of human capital accumulation); and third, it raises labor scarcity for those remaining behind. Of course, there is a fourth and offsetting effect that is often forgotten: it may also crowd out unskilled urban workers already resident there, perhaps pushing them into lower-paying service-sector jobs.

2 What's Wrong with the Conventional Wisdom?

It seems to me that this conventional wisdom gets into trouble when it pushes the first of these sources of poverty reduction too hard – that is, that rural emigration to better urban jobs implies an escape from poverty given wage gaps between farm and city. Kuznets himself used this kind of thinking to attack two related problems associated with the industrial revolution. First, the Kuznets Curve. Second, the sources of accelerating growth from a stagnant agrarian base.

Let me repeat his Kuznets Curve story from Lecture One. It went something like this. Imagine an agrarian society where all farm laborers are poor, earning, let us say, 5 pesos. Let some modernizing influence introduce an urban job offering a wage of 10 pesos, which is first enjoyed by just one lucky rural emigrant. As the pace of industrialization picks up, more such jobs are created and more rural emigrants exploit those opportunities. Eventually, everyone is in the city earning the 10 pesos. Any conventional inequality measure will rise from the initial perfect agrarian equality but eventually it will return to perfect urban equality. This simple model *does*, therefore, trace out a Kuznets Curve, and it also implies that industrialization reduces poverty, the faster the rate of industrialization, the faster the rate of poverty reduction. But the model has some obvious flaws. Why does that city job pay twice as much as the farm job? First, it may be because the city job requires more human capital, and thus requires the migrant to make more investments than simply in the move itself. If so, the escape from rural poverty may be blocked by the inability of the potential migrant to find the resources for the investment. One such constraint on the investment is rural poverty itself and the current income constraint that it implies. We shall have more to say about this in Lecture Three. Second, it may be because some labor market failure has created a gap between these wages. If so, then there is indeed a free lunch awaiting the potential emigrant fleeing rural poverty. There is certainly a long tradition in the development and historical literature that adopts this second view, and we shall have more to say about it in a moment.

Kuznets, Denison, and others have also exploited this line of thinking when searching for the "sources" of growth. Namely, growth can and has been accelerated by eliminating the factor market failure which we assume to be manifested by wage and average labor productivity gaps between farm and industry. Thus, these scholars believe that a good portion of the growth observed in developing economies past and present can be accounted for simply by the elimination of the Harberger Triangles implied by wage gaps. The inference is misleading, to say the least. First, we have to show that average labor productivity gaps cannot be adequately explained by differences in capital intensity, human or non-human. If they can be so explained, then where's the free lunch? Second, if they cannot be so explained, then what is the source of the wage gap? If it is some transitory gap generated by some shock associated with the industrial revolution – like more rapid technological advance in the city, or more rapid accumulation in the city, or greater demographic pressure in the countryside, then shouldn't this source of growth be attributed to the shock itself?

We need to know much more about the magnitude of these wage gaps and the labor market forces that produce them before we can be very confident about the role of emigration as an escape from rural poverty. Even given the wage gaps, it is not enough simply to measure the size of the rural emigrations to identify the process as an escape from rural poverty. We need to go behind those migrations and to understand what's driving them. Urban wage setting, the domestic terms of trade, and government expenditure policy, for example, all have very different implications than do technological progress and accumulation. If technical progress and accumulation dominate, then everyone is likely to gain, both movers and stayers. If an exogenous rise in urban wages, or a price twist, or a government expenditure bias favoring industry dominate, then the rural stayers don't share in the gains. Thus, it is important to isolate what has been important historically in accounting for rural emigration, including the evolution of price policy and the urban bias.

In case I haven't made myself clear, I am appealing for more general equilibrium thinking about the historical evolution of rural emigration. To use old fashioned terms, we need more empirical evidence on the sources of "push and pull." I do *not* have in mind the estimated coefficients on earnings variables in sending and receiving regions – Lord knows that literature is already big enough. Such migration equations tell us nothing about the process of migration from rural poverty since they simply regress one endogenous variable – migration, on another – earnings differentials. What we need instead are ways of thinking about the fundamental labor market forces in city and countryside which push and pull rural emigrants into the cities. These ways of thinking must then be applied to the historical experience of as many countries passing through the industrial revolution as possible. But before I can elaborate on the historical forces of push and pull which draw the rural poor out of poverty during industrial revolutions, we must devote some attention to the wage gaps themselves.

3 Wage Gaps in the Old World: What Was Their Impact?

As I have already stressed, one of the central premises of development economics is that industrialization makes it possible to transfer resources – mainly labor – from low agrarian to high industrial productivity. Most readers will not need to be reminded that the argument was formalized in an elegant way by W. Arthur Lewis (1954) more than thirty years ago. What you may have forgotten about the labor surplus model, however, is that it contains two premises about factor market failure: wage gaps, which make it possible for labor's marginal product to be higher in industry than in agriculture; and capital market imperfections which make it necessary for industrial accumulation to be financed entirely by internally generated funds. The first ingredient is essential since industrialization implies a resource transfer from low-productivity agriculture to high-productivity industry, with resulting national income gains *and* poverty reduction. The second ingredient is essential since, in the absence of those capital market imperfections, the agricultural surplus would be used for industrial accumulation, and an important constraint on industrial accumulation would be released.

What the Lewis model asks, therefore, is: how will an economy evolve through time if it exhibits factor market failure? What it fails to ask, however, is: how would the economy evolve through time if those distortions were absent? Presumably, without the wage distortions rural emigration would be faster, industrial labor costs lower, profits higher, and the rate of accumulation more rapid.

Are the wage gaps we observe true measures of distortions, and if so are they are large enough to matter? Oddly enough, there has been little empirical attention devoted to such questions. My remarks will try to fill that gap. They are based on some research I have done on England during the industrial revolution (Wiliamson, 1987) and America from the 1890s to World War Two (Hatton and Williamson, 1989). While a sample of two hardly warrants a theorem, they offer the best example I know of to illustrate the argument: after all, the labor-surplus model has its roots in British classical tradition, and the classical economists were writing about the economy we are about to analyze; and if the arguments apply to an advanced industrial economy like interwar America, then we might feel more confident with generalization.

A final word of warning: here we shall take measured wage gaps as evidence of true disequilibrium. In the next section, we shall look to historical evidence from America to see whether the disequilibrium characterization is appropriate.

Wage Gaps and Labor Market Failure

It turns out that the gap between the annual nominal earnings of unskilled workers in the urban building trades and farm laborers rose sharply across the first half of the nineteenth century in England. With the 1820s, the pace of industrialization accelerated and the derived demand for labor shifted dramatically away from agriculture and towards urban activities. Furthermore, and in contrast with much of the contemporary Third World, the natural rate of labor force growth was far higher in the countryside than in the city. This relative rural demographic glut is explained in part by the fact that fertility rates were higher in the countryside, but mostly by the fact that death rates were higher in the cities in an era when investment in city social overhead was low and the urban health environment debilitating. In any case, demographic forces placed far greater pressure on English labor markets since the excess rural labor supplies and excess urban labor demands posed a greater challenge to rural emigration as a force for clearing these two labor markets. If labor market disequilibrium was ever to appear during an industrial revolution, the times were certainly ripe for it during those decades of early English industrialization. The wage gap would appear to reflect those disequilibrium forces since it rose sharply to 1851. The gap never regained that mid nineteenth-century peak thereafter. If we are looking for evidence of labor market failure, the 1830s, 1840s, and 1850s are clearly the place to start.

How big was the wage gap in the 1830s? In the south of England, it was very large indeed, about 106 percent (table 2.1). In the north of England, it was smaller, about 36 percent. Elsewhere I have offered some explanations for the regional difference in the size of these wage gaps, but it should suffice here simply to note that a weighted average of the two regions yields an all-England nominal wage gap of about 73 percent.

Since all industrializing countries find it difficult to cope with the economic shocks associated with industrial revolutions, wage gaps are a manifestation of factor market disequilibrium that both economic historians and development economists have come to expect during such episodes of dramatic economic transformation. What matters, therefore, is a comparative assessment: did English labor markets fail by the standards of other industrial revolutions?

Ever since Kuznets and Lewis guessed that the wage gap was typically 30 percent, economists have been busy gathering hard evidence. Table 2.1 collects some of the results. Lyn Squire (1981) documented wage gaps of about 41 percent in 19 Third World economies in the 1960s and 1970s, and Colin Clark (1957) found them to have been about 51 percent among late nineteenth-century industrializers. While it is not presented in table 2.1, the wage gap in America in the 1890s was also about 50 percent. It appears that wage gaps were unusually large in England during the First Industrial Revolution just as a disequilibrium model would have predicted.

Table 2.1 Nominal Wage Gaps for Unskilled
Labor: Some Comparative Data

Observation	Wage Gap (%)
South of England 1830s	106.2
North of England 1830s	36.3
All England 1830s	73.2
Third World 1960s–70s	41.4
Late nineteenth-century Industrializers	51.2

Source: Williamson (1987, Table 3)

Nominal wage gaps are one thing, real wage gaps are another, and economists have been pretty casual about reconciling the difference. What matters, of course, is the latter. After adjusting for the fact that cities were expensive, that cities were environmentally unattractive and required some compensation for the "bads" prevailing there, and that poor relief was used to augment workers' incomes in the countryside during the slack season, a good share of the large English wage gap *does* disappear. Whereas the nominal wage gap was 73 percent for England as a whole, the real wage gap was considerably less, about 33 percent – remarkably close to the Kuznets and Lewis guess of 30 percent. Much of the nominal wage gap *was* illusory, but it hardly disappears even when it is measured properly. Labor market failure *was* an attribute of the First Industrial Revolution.

Migration Response

Rural emigration appears to have responded to the labor market disequilibrium associated with the industrialization spurt after about 1820. Table 2.2 shows that the rate of emigration from the English countryside rose dramatically up to the 1840s. These emigration rates were high by almost any standard. They ranged between about 0.9 and 1.6 percent per annum after 1816, whereas they never exceeded about 1.2 percent per annum in the Third World in the 1960s and 1970s. More important to the issues at hand, however, the rate of rural emigration rose sharply over the period, following the wage gap trends. By the 1840s the emigration rate was almost three times the rate in the 1810s.

The 1830s seem to lie in the midst of a dramatic epoch of high and rising emigration from the countryside at precisely the time when wage gaps were also high and rising, thus offering a strong inducement to potential migrants. However, the migrants' response was apparently insufficient to eliminate or even reduce the wage gap between city and countryside.

Table 2.2 Rural Emigration Rates in England and Wales,
1811–1861

Period	Rural Population at Starting Year (000)	Rural Emigration Over Five Years (000)	Annual Rates of Rural Emigration (%)
1811–16	6,268	181	0.59
1816–21	6,572	281	0.87
1821–6	6,895	397	1.19
1826–31	7,174	399	1.14
1831–6	7,339	364	1.01
1836–41	7,575	442	1.20
1841–6	7,740	583	1.57
1846–51	7,776	646	1.73
1851–6	7,699	571	1.54
1856–61	7,745	594	1.60

Source: Williamson (1987, p. 50)

Deadweight Losses: A Partial Equilibrium Assessment

Were these wage gaps quantitatively significant? How badly
did English factor markets fail? If there had been a more
nearly optimal allocation of labor in England in the 1830s,
would national income have been raised considerably, would
industrializaiton have taken place much more rapidly, and
would rural emigration have been even more dramatic? Any
answer would, of course, assume that the wage gaps reflect
disequilibrium. They may not. But before we confront
efficiency wage advocates and the equilibrium wage gap view,
it makes sense to see first whether it matters.

The proposition is explored by implementing the analysis
underlying figure 2.1, just like Harvey Leibenstein (1957),
and Chris Dougherty and Marcelo Selowsky (1973) did for
some Third World economies a while ago. This familiar
diagram shows employment distribution between agriculture
and industry in the presence of wage gaps. As we shall see,
the partial equilibrium assumptions of figure 2.1 are much

too simple for serious empirical analysis, but given the two derived labor demand functions, the conventionally measured deadweight loss associated with wage gaps – sometimes called the Harberger Triangle – can be computed as the shaded area.

What do we find when this simple partial equilibrium analysis is applied to England in the 1830s? The deadweight loss turns out to be about 0.5 percent of national income, a tiny number, much like those typically found in the applied public finance and labor economics literature. It hardly seems possible to develop a case for English labor market failure on the basis of such tiny numbers. A corollary is that any improvement in labor markets after the 1830s cannot have contributed much to growth performance over the remainder

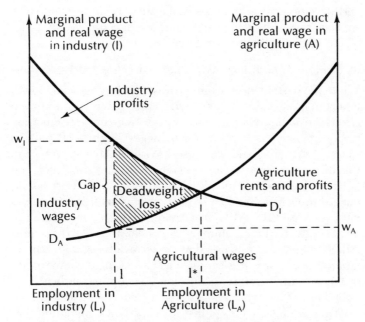

Figure 2.1 "Partial" general equilibrium analysis of wage gaps in two sectors.

of the century – Simon Kuznets and sources of growth practitioners notwithstanding. This is worth emphasizing. In a series of publications on the sources of growth, Edward Denison (1967; Denison and Chung, 1976) argued that the reallocation of labor after World War Two contributed in large measure to rapid growth in Japan and in much of Europe. The English evidence suggests the contrary. If the labor market disequilibrium generated by the industrial revolution implied only a tiny deadweight loss, how could the elimination of that loss contribute much to growth thereafter? And if England in the 1830s had wage gaps greater than those of the Third World, the elimination of labor market distortions is unlikely to matter much in contemporary Asia, Africa, or Latin America either.

If labor market failure during industrial revolutions did not cost the average citizen much, why do economic historians and development economists make such a fuss over it? Have we been misled by the partial equilibrium comparative statics of the deadweight loss literature?

A General Equilibrium Assessment of Labor Market Failure

While the partial equilibrium deadweight loss associated with labor market failure was trivial, the general equilibrium effects, distributional incidence, and long-run accumulation responses may have been much bigger. Figure 2.2 tells us exactly who gains and who loses. With the disappearance of the distortion, wages would have risen in agriculture and fallen in industry. It follows that rents in agriculture would have diminished (by EHGF) and profits in industry would have increased (by ABHC). Laborers gain in agriculture but lose in industry for an ambiguous net change of DGFE minus ABDC. Figure 2.2 suggests that simple deadweight loss calculations may be very misleading when assessing the importance of labor market failure on income distribution, industrialization, and accumulation. To the extent that the classical saving postulate holds, industrial captial accumulation was significantly choked off by those wage gaps. That is, if the reinvestment rate was far higher out of industrial profits than

out of agricultural rents, then aggregate savings were lower
in the presence of labor market failure, and so too must have
been the rate of accumulation economy-wide. Even if the
classical saving postulate did not hold, imperfect capital markets would have ensured that the rate of accumulation in
industry would have been lower, given the lower profits in the
presence of labor market failure. It follows that the rate of
urban job creation for potential rural emigrants would have
been lower too.

The best way to seek answers to these questions is by
appealing to computable general-equilibrium (CGE) models.
One of the main attributes of the CGE model used here
is that capital is allowed to chase after labor even though
institutional distortions are assumed to restrict mobility in

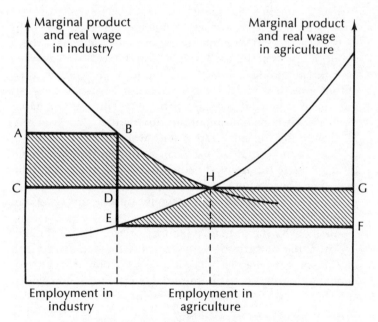

*Figure 2.2 "Partial" general equilibrium analysis of wage
gaps: who gains and who loses?*

this factor market too. Those who tend to be suspicious of CGE models may be appeased by the news that this one tracks British macro-history between 1820 and 1860 very well. Furthermore, the long-run CGE model yields very different results compared with the short-run partial equilibrium model. Here they are.

First, the deadweight losses associated with labor market failure are six to seven times as great, primarily because capital is allowed to chase after labor in the general equilibrium case. Second, the results suggest that industrial employment must have been seriously choked off by those wage gaps. While England's industrialization performance was certainly impressive, it would have been far more impressive in the absence of those distortions. Indeed, I estimate that industrial employment would have been something like 23 percent higher. If that increase is stretched over the two decades 1821 to 1841, it implies that industrial employment growth would have been 3 percent per year, not the 2 percent per year actually achieved. Manufacturing output would have been about 73 percent higher. And if that increase is stretched over the period 1815 to 1841, it implies that manufacturing output growth would have been about 5.2 percent per year, not the 3.1 percent actually achieved. Third, these labor market distortions had important distributional implications. In their absence, industrial profits would have been much higher (by more than 78 percent), at the expense of agricultural rents. If the reinvestment rate out of profits was relatively high, as most of us believe, then the elimination of wage gaps would have resulted in a significant rise in saving and accumulation.

Finally, while labor market failure starved industry of labor, it glutted the countryside with a surplus. In fact, the agricultural labor force may have been too big by more than a third, implying that the escape from rural poverty was not exploited anywhere near fast enough, although it held up unskilled wages in the city. The net impact of the labor market failure on the unskilled in the bottom 40 percent was tiny in the short-run: it simply influenced their location. The influence was far greater in the long-run since it significantly suppressed the rate of accumulation and job creation in industry.

4 Wage Gaps in the New World: What Explains Them?

As we turn from the old world to the new, let's add two additional questions to the agenda. First, do these wage gaps reflect true disequilibrium between city and countryside? Second, why would so many of the rural poor ignore one effective escape from rural poverty? Economists are split into two camps on this issue.

Hagen's Dynamic Distortions

By 1958, the early pioneers in development economics had a full appreciation of wage gaps, and they were central to debates over development strategy. Everett Hagen published an influential paper in that year on "An Economic Justification of Protectionism." Hagen's priors were very strong. He felt that these wage differentials were the result of unbalanced growth in the derived demand for labor. Rapid industrialization creates an excess demand for labor in urban sectors while a lagging agriculture creates an excess supply in rural sectors. Since migration is never adequate to clear these two markets in any one year, and since unbalanced growth persists year in and year out, a wage gap will emerge. The more rapid the rate of unbalanced growth, the bigger the wage gap.

Establishing the argument that wage gaps reflected true wage distortions was central to Hagen's agenda since they helped support a policy of active intervention to foster industrialization. By appealing to wage distortions, Hagen could offer support for the infant industry argument for protection, leaning heavily on the contributions of Haberler and Viner. Since those wage distortions tended to price domestic manufacturers out of their own markets (artificially raising labor costs), government intervention to offset the distortion was warranted.

Unemployment, Todaro, and Equilibrium Wage Gaps
Other economists disagreed, and thought instead that some
omitted variables could account for the wage gap, and further
that the wage gap reflected a labor market equilibrium. One
such omitted variable was unemployment.

W. Arthur Lewis was the first to bring attention to urban
unemployment in the Third World. It appears prominently
in his 1965 Richard T. Ely lecture to the American Economic
Association. Four years later, Michael Todaro (1969)
developed a framework which formalized Lewis's argument.
The Todaro model and its extensions have enjoyed considerably popularity over the two decades which followed. While
I hesitate to elaborate on a model which has had such a long
history in the development literature, there may be some
readers for whom a refresher course might be helpful. The
most effective illustration can be found in Max Corden and
Ronald Findlay (1975), reproduced in figure 2.3. Under the
extreme assumption of wage equalization through migration,
and in the absence of wage rigidities, equilibrium is achieved
at E (the point of intersection of the two labor demand curves,
AA' and MM'). Here wages are equalized at $w_A^* = w_M^*$, and
the share of the total labor force, L, employed in urban jobs
is $O_M L_M^*$, where M denotes manufacturing and A denotes
agriculture. Since, as we have seen, wages are not equalized
in the contemporary Third World, the model incorporates
the widely held belief that the wage rate in manufacturing is
pegged at artificially high levels by unions, minimum wage
legislation, or private-sector emulation of inflated public-sector wage rates, say at $\bar{w}_M$. That is, Todaro introduces an
asymmetry in these two labor markets with wages flexible in
agriculture but fixed in industry – or what Greg Lewis called
the "uncovered" and the "covered" sectors. If, for the moment,
we ignore urban unemployment, then all those who fail to
secure favored jobs in manufacturing would accept low-wage
jobs in agriculture at w_A^{**}. Now let's add the reality of urban
unemployment. Todaro introduces an expectations hypothesis
which, in its simplest form, states that the favored jobs are
allocated by lottery, that the potential migrant calculates the

expected value of that lottery ticket, and compares it with the certain employment in the rural sector. Migration then takes place until the urban expected wage is equated to the rural wage. If the probability of getting the favored job is simply one minus the urban unemployment rate, then the structural equation of migration behavior is the qq' curve in figure 2.3 (which exhibits unitary elasticity). The equilibrium agricultural wage is now given by w_A.

The new equilibrium at Z in figure 2.3 offers an explanation for wage gaps observed between city and countryside which competes with the Hagen hypothesis. While Hagen views these wage gaps as a manifestation of dynamic disequilibrium, Todaro views them as an equilibrium outcome. Who's right? A lot seems to hinge on the answer.

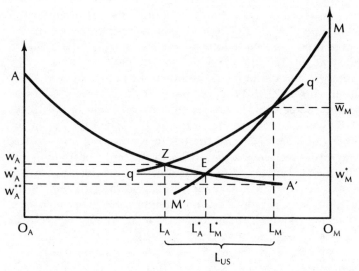

Figure 2.3 The Todaro model according to Corden and Findlay (1975).

American Twentieth-Century Experience with Wage Gaps

Oddly enough, to my knowledge these competing propositions have never been formally tested with time series data. Even more surprising, while the Todaro model was constructed to explain a contemporary Third World problem, the proposition has its intellectual roots with agricultural economists who were writing about the American inter-war wage gap some forty years ago. Todaro himself was aware of this tradition when he cited US experience with exceptionally large wage gaps in the 1930s.

The unskilled wage ratio of farm to city – deflated by cost of living differentials – is plotted in figure 2.4. The variance across the five decades between 1890 and 1941 is striking, and this is the first piece of evidence with which any equilibrium wage model will have to struggle. If the wage gap is to be viewed as an equilibrium wage outcome, why does that equilibrium undergo such wide variation over time (a result we saw repeated a century earlier during the British industrial revolution)? How are we to explain the persistent rise in the wage ratio from the relatively low levels in the mid 1890s to the end of World War One, its dramatic collapse in the immediate post-war years, and then the plunge to even lower levels in the 1930s? Indeed, by 1939 the real wage gap was about 120 percent, far bigger than even Britain in the 1830s.

Of course, it is possible in theory to explain the rise in the interwar wage gap (and the fall in the ratio of farm to city wages) by reference to figure 2.3. If the terms of trade moves sharply against agriculture – as it did world-wide after World War One, then the AA' curve shifts downwards and to the left, the wage gap opens, and urban unemployment increases. If there is a slump in industry while sticky city wages hold up – as was certainly true after 1929, then the MM' curve shifts downwards and to the right, the wage gaps opens, and urban unemployment increases. If, in fact, the real wage in industry rises – as it did during the deflations of the early 1890s and the 1930s, then, once again, the wage gap opens, and urban unemployment increases. If the shocks persisted, then the wage gap would too. But are these long-run shocks

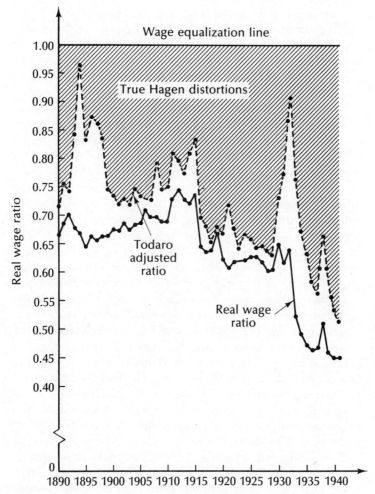

*Figure 2.4 Real wage ratio, Todaro-adjusted real wage ratio,
and true Hagen distortions, 1890–1941.*
Source: Hatton and Williamson (1989, Figure 3)

embedded in an equilibrium model likely to account for the enormous increase in the wage gap observed? Indeed, any equilibrium model – like Todaro's – will have to explain why it is that the wage gap is still large even after accounting for both cost of living differences *and* urban unemployment experience. When such crude adjustments are made in figure 2.4, "true Hagen wage distortions" persist, and they became increasingly large as time wore on over the five decades.

Tim Hatton and I recently sought answers to these questions by translating the structural equations underlying figure 2.3 into a reduced form model which also introduced lags into migration responses to labor market signals (Hatton and Williamson, 1989). When Todaro's structural equation is explored by itself, the results suggest that urban unemployment did indeed help drive the wage gap. But the adjustment lags were very long so that a disequilibrium wage gap could persist for at least half a decade. And when Todaro's structural equation is embedded in the complete model, the shocks driving both the wage gap and urban unemployment can be identified. There were three fundamental shocks which did most of the work: the agricultural terms of trade (which collapsed after World War One), shifts in the derived demand for industrial labor (associated with the interwar business cycle and the global industrial crisis of the 1930s), and urban real wage shocks (associated with sticky nominal wages in industrial employment, and inversely correlated with shifts in the derived demand for industrial labor). The stop and go of foreign immigration into American cities also played a secondary role in crowding out and crowding in the rural emigrants.

Three main morals emerge from this story. First, wage gaps even for an advanced economy like the USA reflect true disequilibrium forces. Rural emigration exhibited a very inelastic response to market signals in the short run and medium term, making it possible for wage gaps to persist over very long periods even after adjusting for the presence of urban unemployment. Second, these two labor markets do indeed exhibit an asymmetry just as Todaro suggested–sticky wages in industry and flexible wages in agriculture. Contemporaries were right in viewing the rural sector as an "industrial labor reserve" such that the urban sector could draw on rural labor supplies when times were good, sending them back in a slump, thus forcing the wage adjustment on agriculture.

The bottom line is that there were two key macro-shocks which created the persistent Hagen-like wage distortions in America during the interwar decades: intersectoral terms of trade shocks driven by world commodity markets, and the derived industrial labor demand shocks driven by industrial crisis.

5 What Drives Rural Emigration in the Long Run?

Regardless of the position taken in the equilibrium versus disequilibrium debate, we need to sort out the underlying determinants of rural emigration in the long run. And regardless of the model of migration preferred, the central question lurking behind all city growth and rural emigration debates in the contemporary Third World is, and in early nineteenth-century Britain was, the quantitative importance of the underlying forces pushing and pulling rural migrants to the city. Over the long haul of the industrial revolution, which forces were doing most of the work? And how were the poor affected by them?

Push and Pull: A Menu of Forces

Three forces have been stressed by both historians and development economists. First, there is Michael Lipton's (1976) pro-urban policy bias, manifested primarily by a shift in the domestic areas of trade against agriculture, stressed long ago by Theodore Schultz and others since. Second, there is unbalanced technological advance favoring industry, and accommodated by rapid rates of urban accumulation, central to the arguments in Lecture One. Third, there are Malthusian forces which create rural labor surplus, forcing rural emigrants into urban employment. There are other forces which have attracted the historians' attention, but it turns out that

their impact in the past has only been very modest. Let me
list three that have been especially visible in the debates:
exogenous increases in agricultural capital intensity and rural
institutional events during green revolutions of the past which
push rural labor into the cities – a force stressed by Marx
when commenting on the English enclosures; a pro-urban
bias in capital allocation, stressed by Lipton – but absent from
the experience of most nineteenth-century industrializers; and
increasing rural land scarcity stressed by all.

The three forces listed at the start seem to be the ones
which have mattered. However, while they have similar implications for rural emigration and city immigration, they have
very different implications for trends in living standards for
the rural and urban poor. Let's consider the two supply-side
forces first, unbalanced total factor productivity advance and
Malthusian pressures.

While such supply-side forces are likely to be at the heart
of city growth and rural emigration experience, demand is
hardly irrelevant, although it is price elasticities that matter,
not income elasticities and Engel's Law. After all, if output
demand is relatively price elastic, then sectoral total factor
productivity growth tends to generate an elastic supply
response rather than a relative price decline. This distinciton
is important since cost-reducing innovations will be passed
on to users by falling prices in the inelastic demand case.
Thus, the rise in the marginal physical product of factors
used in a technologically dynamic sector will be partially
offset by price declines, so that marginal value products rise
by less, and resource shifts may also be less, and this includes
labor. If, on average, urban sectors tend to have relatively
high rates of total factor productivity growth, and if the
demand for urban output is relatively price elastic, then
final demand shifts towards the dynamic sectors, the derived
demand for urban employment is augmented, urban job vac-
ancies are created, rural emigration responds, and city growth
takes place. The higher are the price elasticities of demand
for urban output, the greater is the city growth and migration
impact of unbalanced productivity advance favoring the mod-

ern sectors. The more open is the economy to foreign trade, the more likely will these conditions be satisfied. The urban and rural poor both gain in the process: good jobs are created in the city which rural emigrants can exploit, real wages rise in the city, real wages also rise in the countryside as the out-migration creates more labor scarcity there, and poor rural cultivators also gain since the terms of trade shifts in their favor.

The strength of these benign urban technological forces will have an important influence on our interpretation of who gains from growth. Consider, for example, the debate on what has been called "overurbanization," initiated by Bert Hoselitz in the 1950s (Hoselitz, 1957). His thesis was that urbanization was outpacing industrialization in developing countries in the sense that urban population shares were large in relation to industrial employment shares, at least when compared with the nineteenth-century historical performance of currently developed countries. He concluded that there must be some forces operating in the contemporary Third World which are pushing rural labor into the cities faster than they can be absorbed in the good industrial jobs, swelling the ranks of the low-wage informal urban service sectors. The obvious candidate for the rural push is the unusual Malthusian pressure associated with the much more rapid rates of population growth accompanying today's industrial revolutions compared with those of the nineteenth century.

Rural emigration can hardly be taken as an indicator of rapid escape from rural poverty if Malthusian forces are doing all the work. After all, it implies a labor glut in urban and rural labor markets and declining living standards among the poor in both. Of course, things would be worse for the rural poor if for some reason they were unable to flee the rural glut, but the empirical issue of importance is whether rapid rates of rural emigration then and now are driven by Malthusian demographic transitions associated with industrial revolutions. Indeed, popular accounts of Third World migration and city growth often suggest that high rates of population growth lie at the core of the problem. While the assertion sounds plausible, this conventional wisdom has not been adequately tested until recently.

Finally, what about the terms of trade between city and countryside? The relative price of urban manufactures has drifted downwards during the past three decades, although the decline was far less dramatic in the 1960s and early 1970s when Third World city growth and rural emigration rates were especially rapid. But how much of that terms of trade movement was driven by dynamic technological and accumulation forces in the Third World itself, forces favoring city production? How much of it was driven by exogenous world market conditions? We need the answers to sort out its influence on rural emigration and the living standards of the poor. In any case, trends in the terms of trade facing agriculture may have had a less important impact historically than the wedge which domestic policy typically has driven between internal and external prices. What role has the anti-agriculture price twist played over the past century anyway?

Some Historical Evidence

Three computable general equilibrium models have been used recently to address these topics historically. First, Allen Kelley and I constructed one to confront the experience of a group of 40 developing countries in the 1960s and 1970s (Kelley and Williamson, 1984). Second, Charles Becker, Edwin Mills, and I have done the same for India from 1960 to 1980 (Becker, Williamson, and Mills, forthcoming). Third, I have recently finished a similar project assessing Britain's experience during the First Industrial Revolution (Williamson, 1990). The limits of space make it impossible to do much more here than simply hint at the findings, but let's give it a try. Consider first the more recent industrial revolutions in the post World War Two Third World.

Which forces mattered most in the Third World during the 1960s and early 1970s? Was arable land scarcity an important ingredient of Third World rural emigration and city growth? The answer coming from counterfactual analysis is an unambiguous no. Have the high rates of population growth been – in the World Bank's terms – the single most important factor distinguishing present from past experience with rural emigration and city growth? Once again, the answer is an unambiguous no. Had the Third World experienced the much lower population growth rates that prevailed in the industrial economies in the 1960s, the rate of city growth would have still been very high, much higher, for example, than in Britain during the First Industrial Revolution.

What about the pace and character of technological progress? In spite of the conventional appeal to Engel's Law and overall rates of productivity growth, it turns out that it is the *unbalanced* character of that productivity growth – and the urban accumulation that accommodated it – which has done most of the work in the past and is likely to do so in the future. The unbalanced rate of technological process in the Third World was the key condition accounting for the unusually rapid rates of rural emigration and city growth in the 1960s and 1970s. The same was true of Britain during her period of dramatic and rising rural emigration across the first half of the nineteenth century. Furthermore, manufacturing has been the key engine driving rural emigration and city growth in the Third World, and the parameters linking manufacturing's performance and rural emigration were much the same in Britain more than a century ago as they are in the Third World today. Indeed, they were even the same in India between 1960 and 1980, a country that suffered a poor performance in manufacturing, and also exhibited slow city growth and relatively low rates of rural emigration. The engine of growth simply failed there, although the engine has run far faster in the 1980s.

I should note, by the way, that the much-maligned urban informal service sector plays a critical role in these historical accounts. It is simply bad economic history to describe them as some residual activity whereby disappointed rural emigrants are dumped into some informal service sector by Marxian reserve. Rather, the sector has served as an important supplier both of city building activities as well as satisfying consumption and intermediate demands generated by the employed resources in the more splashy modern sectors.

Finally, exogenous changes in the terms of trade between city and countryside played an important role in conditioning the rural emigration rate. This is one critical reason why rural emigration rates were so high in the 1960s and early 1970s in the Third World. They would have been lower, of course, had not agriculture in the Third World been subjected to an anti-agriculture policy price twist in the terms of trade. And the lower rural emigration rate would *not* have implied more modest rates of escape from rural poverty, but rather an enhancement of the rate of escape *within* the rural sector itself. Has this anti-agriculture price policy always been a fact of history? Or does the contemporary Third World conform to some historical law of policy intervention?

6 Policy Intervention and Price Twist

Every development economist is acutely aware of the pro-urban bias embedded in Third World development strategies, strategies which are manifested in particular by a policy price twist unfavorable to agriculture. Development economists reading these lectures may be less familiar with the fact that this strategy is fully consistent with the past century or more of historical experience with industrial revolutions. It is not idiosyncratic to the Third World, but rather generic of most industrial revolutions. If development analysts were better acquainted with this fact of history, they might be less frustrated by their inability to change it.

The Historical Evolution of Anti-Agriculture Policies

In a recent paper on modern fiscal redistribution, Peter Lindert (1989) has shown that most economies undergoing the industrial revolution evolve from policies which tax export-oriented agriculture to ones which subsidize it. Symmetrically, the favored treatment of import-competing manufacturing declines with development. Lindert also shows that this switch in policy has a close positive correlation with the other modes of fiscal redistribution discussed briefly in Lecture One. There we documented an increase in fiscal progressivity across the twentieth century among the industrialized nations, fiscal trends which themselves correlate with egalitarian trends in pre-fisc incomes generated in the marketplace. Anti-agriculture policies, regressive fiscal policy, and inequality seem to go hand in hand as countries rise to NIC status on the upswing of the Kuznets Curve; they tend to retreat from those policies thereafter when egalitarian trends are set in motion on the downside of the Kuznets Curve.

As Lindert points out, this pattern is revealed by American history. In the first half of the nineteenth century, while America gained about four decades of experience with the industrial revolution, industry received modest levels of tariff protection. Producers of export staples in the cotton south were well aware of the tax which such trade policies implied, but had the political clout to resist. The Civil War eliminated that political clout, and anti-agriculture price-twisting policies persisted for about seven decades until the 1930s. Since then, agriculture has been favored not only by price supports, but also by explicit transfers. A similar policy evolution can be found in Japan's modern history, although anti-agriculture policies appear somewhat earlier in her industrialization experience and take the form of direct taxation rather than of price twist. This was certainly true of Meiji Japan, but farmers were receiving high levels of net protection by the late 1930s, a trend that continued into the post-World War Two period (and frustrates American export interests today). The industrial revolutionary experience of Korea and Taiwan have been far more rapid and thus the switch in policy towards agriculture has been compressed within a shorter time period, evolving from policies in the 1950s which depressed farm prices to policies in the 1980s which support them. Similar tales can be told for France and Germany. Classic industrial protection in the nineteenth century began to erode in the face of agricultural interests in the early twentieth century; aggressive net protection of agriculture arrived in the 1930s; and it was reinforced with heavy subsidies in the post-war period.

What about the leader of the industrial pack, Britain? Here the story is a bit more complex since Britain does not begin her industrial revolution as a primary product exporter. Instead, she starts as a net *importer* of primary products, grains in particular (or what she called "corn"), while exporting manufactures. In this case, the import-competing sector is grain, but its treatment roughly conforms to the historical law emerging. Namely, the import-competing grain sector was heavily protected up to around 1820 following four decades of industrialization; the level of protection persisted, but at lower rates, up to the early 1840s; the 1840s, of course, form an historic benchmark since it was in 1846 that the Corn Laws were repealed, after which Britain opted for free trade. It could be argued that it was the Irish potato famine in the late 1840s which forced a switch in policy from one which taxed the key wage goods – grain and bread, to a more pro-poor free-trade policy which served to eliminate that tax, but such arguments exaggerate the role of the famine. After all, the level of protection and price twist had been falling from the 1820s to the 1840s, so Britain was likely to have adopted free trade about this time anyway. And certainly Britain had reached NIC status by that time; indeed, she was far and away the most industrialized country in the world.

The Impact of Policy Price Twist During Past Industrial Revolutions: Assessing the British Corn Laws

So what was the impact of the Corn Laws during the First Industrial Revolution when inequality was on the rise, and when living standards of the poor were lagging behind? The debates from 1815 to 1846 always posed these issues in distributional terms. The Anti-Corn Law League made it absolutely clear who gained and who lost. Landlords, at the very top of the income pyramid, gained from high rents. Capitalists in manufacturing, somewhere in the middle of the income pyramid, suffered since they had to pay higher nominal wages, their export trade was repressed, and their profits were choked off. Closer to the bottom of the income pyramid, the real wage of urban workers suffered from the "bread tax." The impact on the poorest of the working poor, rural farm laborers, was less clear since the employment impact and the cost of living impact were offsetting. The same ambiguity applied to all workers in the bottom 40 percent. Debate over these magnitudes has been going on now for a century and a half.

General equilibrium models are clearly the best way to assess the Corn Laws or any other price-twist policy associated with early industrial revolutions. When a five-sector, open-economy model is applied to Britain in the 1830s we get some striking answers (Williamson, 1986b). Table 2.3 estimates the impact of the Corn Laws where Ricardo's small country assumption is invoked. That is, the domestic price of tradables is determined exogenously by world market conditions and British tariff policy. The counterfactual supposes that the repeal was passed in the mid 1830s so that the 54 percent tariff on grains is removed all at once. World market conditions, domestic endowments, and technologies are all held constant.

What would have been the impact of an early repeal and the elimination of the price twist? Table 2.3 estimates that 21 percent of the labor force would have fled agriculture in response to deteriorating employment conditions induced by an early repeal. This is clearly a large figure, implying that about a fifth of the agricultural labor force would have been made redundant by a movement towards free trade in the 1830s. The Anti-Corn Law League argued that the tariffs choked off the supply of labor to manufacturing, that the Corn Laws served to suppress the export of manufactures, and thus that actual industrialization was slower than it would have been under free trade. An early repeal, they argued, would have served to augment the supply of labor to manufacturing, to stimulate exports, and to boost the rate of industrialization. According to the Ricardian small country model, it appears that the league was absolutely correct. Indeed, a move to free trade would have augmented

Table 2.3 Estimating the Impact of an Early Repeal of the Corn
Laws Under Ricardian Small Country Assumptions

	%[a]
Employment (Unskilled)	
Agriculture	−21
Industry	+6
Manufacturing	+24
Services (and Mining)	−11
Output (Constant Price)	
Agriculture	−6
Industry	+4
Manufacturing	+22
Services (and Mining)	−13
Rents, Wages and GNP	
Agricultural Rents	−20
Real Unskilled Wage	+23
Nominal	−1
Workers' Cost-of-Living	−25
Real Skilled Wage	+15
Nominal	+1
Workers' Cost-of-Living	−14
Real GNP Per Capita	+2
Income Distribution (Nominal)	
Surplus (Rents and Profits) in Agriculture	−22
Profits in Industry	+1
Profits in Manufacturing	+22
Profits in Services (and Mining)	−13
Manufacturing Exports	
	+246

[a] Figures are rounded.
Source: Williamson (1986b, Table 3)

employment in manufacturing by 24 percent. The figure for industrial employment would have been considerably less, of course, since the large non-tradable urban service sector would have contracted, releasing resources to booming manufacturing. Manufactured exports would have risen by an enormous 246 percent, implying a counterfactual export growth more like 7 percent per annum rather than the rate of 4 percent actually achieved.

Who gained and who lost from Repeal of the Corn Laws? Certainly landlords and tenant farmers lost a great deal. Table 2.3 estimates that the surplus in farm production (rents and profits) would have been cut by 22 percent by an early repeal in the 1830s. Who would have gained? The average Briton would have gained very little: early repeal would have removed the deadweight losses associated with the tariffs, but the gain in real GNP per capita would have been no more than 2 percent. Like most Harberger Triangle calculations, this figure is very small. No wonder the debate over the Corn Laws ignored aggregate income effects. Distributional issues were more central.

Table 2.3 suggests that common labor had a great deal at stake in the debate since the positive effects of removal of the "bread tax" would have swamped the negative employment effects. The net effect of an early repeal in the 1830s would have been to raise unskilled real wages by about 23 percent. If this estimate is even close to the mark, it suggests that the Corn Laws help explain why common labor's standard of living lagged behind in the first half of the nineteenth century. The Corn Laws appear to have squeezed the distribution in the middle a bit. That is, capitalists in manufacturing suffered. Opponents of the Corn Laws believed that it was laborers and capitalists who were paying the subsidy to grain producers, and that industrial profits were significantly augmented by repeal. The estimates in table 2.3 suggest that they were only partially right. Manufacturing profits would have risen by 22 percent in response to an early repeal, but industrial profits would have risen by far less, only 1 percent. Combined with the estimates of the Corn Law's impact on agricultural rents, a good share of the rising inequality during the First Industrial Revolution may be attributable to the Corn Laws.

All of this analysis assumes with Ricardo that the external terms of trade were unaffected by Britain's tariff policy. Torrens disagreed. He thought the tariff improved the external terms of trade enough to overturn these results. However, when the model is expanded to include Torren's position, unskilled labor at the bottom of the distribution still suffer under the Corn Laws.

7 A Summing Up

We have covered a lot of ground. The determinants of rural emigration during industrial revolutions are complex, and it is not always clear that high rates of emigration imply improvements in the human condition of the rural poor at the bottom of the distribution. Yes, urban pull conditions have been doing most of the work since the First Industrial Revolution started in 1780. The key force driving that historical result has been the unbalanced character of technological advance favoring urban activities, manufacturing in particular. The rural poor clearly gain from such forces. Yes, there has been a persistent urban bias during early industrial revolutions, and in the nineteenth century it took the form of price twist against agriculture. It tends to erode as countries pass through NIC status, finally switching to an egalitarian pro-agricultural policy in late stages of development. This evolution of price policy helps explain why so many countries undergo a Kuznets Curve. Yes, there are true disequilibrium wage gaps out there, offering an easy escape from rural poverty. Furthermore, these wage distortions have retarded industrialization and the long-run escape from poverty in important ways. Yet, the key to poverty reduction does not simply lie with rural emigration which exploits the wage gaps. Rather, it lies with technological performance and accumulation within farm and city, the forces which create the wage gaps in the first place.

3

Lecture Three
Accumulation and Inequality: Making the Connection

1 The Smithian Trade-off: Growth Versus Equality

The Rhetoric

It seemed appropriate to include in these Kuznets Memorial Lectures some attention to a very old question: must policy-makers choose between growth and equity?

Certainly the British classical economists thought so. For at least two centuries, mainstream economists and those making policy were guided by the belief that the national product could not be raised while at the same time giving the poor a larger share. After all, did not redistribution to the poor diminish the surplus for saving and accumulation? Furthermore, in the 1950s and 1960s the premise became firmly embedded in modern versions of the classical model, like those associated with Sir Arthur Lewis (1954), and John Fei and Gus Ranis (1964). Indeed, Lewis thought that the central problem during industrial revolutions was increasing the net saving rate from something like 5 percent to something like 15 percent, and that one key source was the rise in the profits share – that is, a shift in the distribution of income.

This view of the trade-off was rarely based on hard evidence or policy experimentation, but rather on theory, allegation, and, it turns out, spurious historical correlation. And since income, wealth, and political clout have always gone together, policies untested during past industrial revolutions were more likely to have been those which might have produced egalitarian growth. Indeed, since only the top economic classes had political voice and literacy in eighteenth and early nineteenth century Britain as well as in most of the rest of Europe, policy tended to be regressive, and the conventional trade-off view reigned supreme. From Adam Smith onwards, therefore, economic thought eulogized saving and attacked generous poor relief. The trade-off has made its way into the late twentieth century: contemporary politicians in the industrialized nations appear to believe that scarce domestic savings is at the heart of the productivity slowdown, and that generous welfare programs somehow account for some of both. Even such critics of capitalism as Marx, Hobson, and Kaldor accepted the classical or Smithian postulate that the rich save a lot more at the margin, and that this fact accounts for aggregate accumulation performance.

With the spread of suffrage in late nineteenth and early twentieth century, the idea began to wane in the advanced economies, all of whom also began to undergo an egalitarian leveling of incomes. With the spread of national independence and rapid growth in the Third World, rejection of the Smithian trade-off gained momentum under the leadership of Robert McNamara and some World Bank economists like Irma Adelman, Hollis Chenery, and Montek Ahluwalia. Their competing view was that much of the Third World had overlooked a vast range of policy options that could have enhanced growth by raising the value of the poor's assets: investments in public health, mass education, rural infrastructure, and staple foods. These prescriptions are now backed by recent historical evidence from the virtuous East Asians, who have been most active in applying them, in contrast with the bad Latins, who have not.

The debate is hardly over, and there are at least two reasons why the controversy is likely to continue over the next two centuries as well. First, highly politicized debates tend to have long lives. Government policies which involve a potential redistribution create opposing self-interests, and each side will promote its cause by economic arguments that are hard to falsify. Second, and more central to the theme of these lectures, the issue is exceedingly difficult to resolve with historical evidence. Certainly the trade-off cannot be assessed by yet another simple statistical regression between growth and inequality. The dynamics of the industrial revolution are much too complex to generate much insight from such simple correlations. Nor can the trade-off be assessed by correlations between inequality, aggregate domestic saving rates, and accumulation, although the nineteenth century certainly offers no shortage of convenient examples. For example, we saw in Lecture One that American inequality rose sharply over the eight decades following 1820. At the same time, the net investment share in national product doubled or tripled, and the rate of capital-deepening quadrupled. It is exactly this kind of correlation – rising inequality coinciding with rising saving and accumulation during industrial revolutions, that reinforced the trade-off postulate among classical economists who developed their growth models while the process was underway in Britain between 1780 and 1860.

Could it be that nineteenth-century correlations are spurious, and that some omitted variables account for both rising inequality on the upswing of the Kuznets Curve and for rising saving rates and accumulation? It is important that we find out since the trade-off view of history still creeps into economic debate in the contemporary Third World. No doubt long-time skeptics are likely to expect a revisionist rejection of this old chestnut in this lecture. After all, twentieth-century histories fail to confirm the correlation. Indeed, the correlation appears to have disappeared even from British and American experience: while the growth rate has been higher in the twentieth century than in the nineteenth, inequality has declined. As Lecture One suggested, the same appears to have been true of France, Germany, and most other members of the OECD.

Before we proceed, I must make some final introductory points to clear the underbrush. As the Third World debate on this issue subsided in the late 1970s and attention shifted to problems of macro-stabilization and debt, development economists therefore failed to pay much attention to the evidence which economic historians had been accumulating on the trade-off in the past. Apart from the shift in interest, there are two additional reasons why the debate may have subsided over the past decade or so. First, the contemporary evidence has persuaded some that domestic saving (whether swollen by rising inequality or not) is not a critical constraint on accumulation – an issue we will confront here at length. Second, the "sources of growth" literature has led many to doubt that accumulation matters that much anyway. I believe, however, that this sources-of-growth literature is grossly misleading. After all, there is a lot of historical evidence suggesting that the mode of accumulation has shifted in the twentieth century away from conventional and towards human capital, and we measure the latter very badly. This shift in the mode of accumulation has been noted by many economists: for example, Paul Schultz (1987) and Richard Easterlin (1981) have both stressed a revolution in mass education: Schultz finding it in the post-World War Two period, with Easterlin finding it even earlier, in the late nineteenth century. Furthermore, the classic debates over the trade-off have typically underplayed human capital. This narrow focus has been unfortunate, since it is here that we might get both equality and growth. While this line of thinking is hardly novel, I believe it is important to look at the historical evidence to support it.

The Argument

Changes in the distribution of income have long been thought to change saving in three ways: first, redistribution toward high-savers generated by events in the market place; second, fiscal policies which do the same; and third, the saving incentives or disincentives generated by diminished or increased taxation on returns to capital. The second and third influences are more recent. The twentieth-century expansion of government tax and transfer activity clearly contributed to the post-fisc egalitarian trend in the industrialized world noted in Lecture One. Many economists suspect that this fiscal redistribution retarded capital formation and productivity growth. Still others insist that capital income taxation has discouraged private saving. However, economic histories from nineteenth-century industrial revolutions have more to say about the first influence, since fiscal action of any sort was modest before the twentieth century.

The first influence is governed, of course, by marginal saving rates. Any market force which redistributes income to the rich may raise aggregate saving and foster accumulation if the rich have higher saving rates at the margin than the poor. Since the rich were always thought to have higher marginal saving rates than the poor, as in Kaldor's or Lewis's famous models, it seemed natural to infer that any redistribution toward the rich would raise domestic saving and accumulation rates. While intuitively plausible and a staple in political economy since Adam Smith, pre-fisc redistribution from poor to rich appears to have had little quantitative impact on the aggregate domestic saving rate. So say studies by Alan Blinder (1980) on post-war United States, by William Cline (1972) on Latin America, or by Philip Musgrove (1980) on international cross-sections. As we shall see, the same is true of nineteenth-century America and Britain on the upswing of their Kuznets Curves. After all, the augmented national saving rate is the product of two small fractions: the share that has been taken from one income class and given to another, and the difference in marginal saving rates between the classes. The resulting changes in the aggregate saving rate are typically too small to assign much importance to the trade-off between equality and accumulation.

But even big redistributions that shift the domestic saving function substantially outward may only have a limited impact on accumulation. After all, the more elastic is the saving response to the rate of return, the less important is *any* of those saving-supply-driven forces which receive so much attention in the historical and the contemporary literature. This includes the modern social security debate in the industrial economies, the demographic dependency-rate debate in the Third World, and, of course, the trade-off debate motivated by the Kuznets Curve across industrial revolutions. What do we know about the response of saving to the rate of return? Our quantitative impressions about the elasticity of domestic saving with respect to the after-tax rate of return are generally higher now than they were a decade or so ago, either for twentieth-century America or for nineteenth-century Britain, the latter supplied by Michael Edelstein (1982). And if *domestic* saving is responsive to the rate of return, *total* saving will be more so in a world of even partially integrated international capital markets.

Furthermore, the more elastic is the saving function, the more important is the investment demand side. While development economists are familiar with the saving-constrained and investment demand-driven debates of the 1970s, I feel the point deserves stress. It may seem easier to explain capital formation from the saving-supply side, given the well-developed literature on the trade-off, the life-cycle, or the dependency-burden. But the approach depends critically on the assumptions that the saving supply function is very inelastic and the investment demand function is very elastic. The direct link between shifts in the saving function and capital accumulation is seriously weakened in those historical circumstances where these assumptions are violated.

Competing Assets and Portfolios

The direct link between income distribution, domestic private saving, and conventional capital formation is further weakened by the availability of competing forms of wealth. The motivation for saving can be served equally well by accumulating government debt, foreign debt, land, slaves, or even property rights, as well as capital gains on any of these. The larger and more elastic are these alternative asset supplies, the stronger are the arguments just made, since conventional capital formation will depend less on shifts in the supply of domestic saving, and more on investment demand.

Of these competing assets, the supply of net foreign debt

is likely to be the most elastic. The more open a nation becomes to international capital flows, the less relevant is the supply of domestic saving to the rate of capital formation. If a nation is a price taker in international financial markets and faces no credit rationing, then domestic capital formation is determined solely by investment demand at home, and distribution effects will not matter at all. Capital formation is determined on the production side in such cases, and domestic saving is irrelevant. Nor is this argument about world capital markets any less compelling for the nineteenth century than for the present. Indeed, recent research by Larry Neal (1985) and Robert Zevin (1989) suggests that world capital markets were no less perfectly integrated in the nineteenth or even the eighteenth century than they were in the 1980s.

The debate over the potential crowding out effect of government debt on capital formation has, of course, raged in the literature for two decades, spilling over into the economic history journals. The facts are that capital formation rates were low in America during the 1860s when debt was issued to finance the Civil War, they were low in England during the French wars up to 1815 or so when debt was also issued to finance those conflicts, and they were low in Meiji Japan during the conflicts with China and Russia from the mid 1890s to the mid 1900s. To the extent that crowding out effects were powerful during these important episodes of early industrialization, then they can swamp the role of income distribution on capital formation and accumulation.

If one believes that different kinds of wealth compete for shares of household portfolios tied to desired wealth–income ratios, then it seems clear that capital gains on land would induce households to accumulate less claims on reproducible capital. Furthermore, we have come to expect capital gains on scarce land to be especially large during episodes of rapid accumulation of other assets in more elastic supply. Thus, urban and rural land values soared during past industrial revolutions. To give a more modern example, real capital gains on land sites have been very large in post-war Japan, running at 16 percent per annum between 1955 and 1974. More importantly, while the saving rate was rising in postwar Japan, those annual capital gains on land sites were falling to about a third in the 1970s of what they were in the 1950s. While there are some notable exceptions, why has so little been written about the potential impact of capital gains in land on accumulation in other forms?

2 Saving and Inequality in Nineteenth-century America: A Spurious Correlation?

Thus, there are lots of reasons to believe that the link between inequality and accumulation is weak. Theory is one thing, however, and fact is another. What does history tell us?

One of the best examples is offered by the American industrial revolution across the nineteenth century (Williamson, 1979). Table 3.1 establishes that the early nineteenth century launched the American economy along a sharply rising trend in accumulation rates. Prior to 1805, nonhuman-wealth accumulation rates were very modest, around 0.2 percent per annum in per capita terms. While the pace quickened up to 1835, the biggest leap took place between 1835 and the end of the Civil War decade. The trend acceleration continued – but at retarding rates – until the turn of the century, after which the pace settled down to a sedate level not unlike the first three decades of the nineteenth century. Associated with this accumulation performance was a rise in the current price gross saving share in GNP. By the early 1840s, that share was already 16 percent, but it surged to 28 percent by the turn of the century. As Table 3.2 shows, the rise in the saving rate was even greater in constant prices since the relative price of investment goods declined over the century. Indeed, the relative price of investment goods declined by 21 percent between 1849 and 1874, a quarter century of dramatic unbalanced total factor productivity growth centered on the capital goods sector, and a period when the gross investment share almost doubled, from 13 percent to 23 percent. This in spite

Table 3.1 Wealth per Capita and Capital per Worker: Growth
Rates, United States, 1685–1966 (% per annum)

Period	Private Physical Wealth per Capita (1967 $) (1)	Depreciable Capital per Laborer (1860 $) (2)	Reproducible Capital per Man-Hour (1860 $) (3)
1685–1805	0.23	–	–
1800–35	–	–	0.77
1835–50	–	–	1.60
1805–50	1.60	–	–
1840–50	–	2.17	–
1855–71	–	–	2.85
1850–1900	1.90	2.63	–
1900–66	1.20	–	–
1900–58	–	1.00	–

Source: Williamson (1979, Table 1, p. 232)

of the fact that demand shifted towards investment goods,
offsetting the supply-side productivity effects. And the relative
price decline would, no doubt, be even bigger were we able
to better control for quality changes.

In net terms, the constant price saving rate doubled or
tripled over the six decades between 1839 and 1897, from
5.9 percent to 15.5 percent (col. 3). Indeed, the rise seems to
replicate Lewis's famous dictum that the central problem of
development economics is to explain the rise in the net savings
rate from 5 percent to 15 percent during industrial revolutions. Meanwhile, the net return on conventional reproducible assets fell from 10.5 percent in the 1800–1835 period to
6.6 percent around the turn of the century.

What accounts for the impressive rise in the American
saving rate from the late 1830s to the turn of the century?
The rise in American inequality discussed at length in Lecture
One offers one possible answer. Indeed, it is precisely this

Table 3.2 Gross and Net Real Investment Shares in the United
States, 1817–1897 (%)

| Year or Period | Gross Investment Share | | Net Investment Share | | Relative Price of Investment Goods Gallman (1860 = 100) |
	Gallman (1)	Gallman-Davis-David (2)	Gallman (3)	Gallman-Davis-David (4)	(5)
1800–35 (1817)	–	11	–	7.9	–
1834–43 (1839)	10	–	5.9	–	107.7
1839–48 (1844)	11	–	6.5	–	107.0
1844–53 (1849)	13	–	7.9	–	103.4
1849–58 (1854)	15	–	9.2	–	95.0
(1859)	–	–	–	–	98.0
1869–78 (1874)	23	–	13.7	–	82.3
1874–83 (1879)	21	–	10.9	–	81.3
1879–88 (1884)	23	–	12.1	–	84.6
1884–93 (1889)	27	–	15.3	–	82.4
1889–98 (1894)	28	–	15.5	–	77.0
1890–1905 (1897)	–	28	–	15.0	73.3

Constant 1860 prices, where cols 1 and 2 refer to the US gross
domestic investment share in gross domestic product.

Source: Williamson (1979, Table 2, p. 233)

kind of gross historical correlation which has been used to
help justify the conclusion that the investment requirements
of early industrialization can only be satisfied by the surplus
generated by rising inequality. So, did increasing American
inequality beget increasing capital formation? Without the
rise in inequality, would American growth have been choked
off?

One can get an answer by implementing the simple model

discussed a moment ago, now embedded in figure 3.1. The saving rate is written on the horizontal axis where real net saving (or investment) shares in GNP are measured. The rise from A to E roughly corresponds to the more than doubling in the net real saving rate from 6 percent or 8 percent in the 1830s to 15 percent or 16 percent at the turn of the century. The decline in the net rate of return on reproducible capital, from r_0 to r_1, roughly corresponds to the observed fall over the same time period. We allow some positive slope to the saving function so that a rise in net rates of return induces additional savings, but the elasticity is kept small since there is no econometric evidence supporting the elastic view.

Suppose the investment demand function shifted to the right in response to the two basic forces which Lecture One argued could account for the rise in inequality. First, the rate

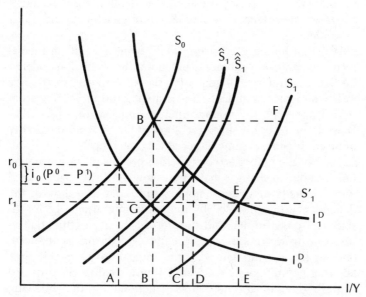

Figure 3.1 American nineteenth-century shifts in investment and saving behavior.

of labor-force growth rose. According to Stanley Lebergott, the labor force grew at about 2.7 percent per annum between 1800 and 1835. The rate accelerated in the middle third of the century when it reached 3.3 percent per annum. There is reason to believe that this trend acceleration fostered a rise in accumulation rates during the first half of the century by shifting investment demand to the right, raising the net rate of return, and inducing increased net saving rates. Labor force growth will not, however, help us explain the continued outward shift in investment demand later in the century since, as is well known, labor force growth declined after the Civil War. Second, the investment demand function shifted to the right in response to an increased rate of labor-saving and capital-using technical change. Lecture One argued that the increasing rate of labor-saving technical change was generated primarily by unbalanced technological progress favoring capital-intensive sectors. It had two effects: it tended to foster inequality, and it raised the aggregate demand for investment goods as those sectors using a lot of machines and skills expanded.

We shall be more precise in identifying the shift in investment demand in a moment, but note the predictions offered by figure 3.1. First, saving rates rise in response to the rise in investment demand, the investment ratio increasing from A to B. Second, the saving function shifts to the right from B to F in response to three forces: the rise in inequality induced by those same labor-saving technical change and rapid unskilled labor force growth forces; a shift in the saving function due to changes in attitudes toward thrift, institutional improvements in savings mobilization, and a decline in the dependency rate induced by foreign immigration which self-selected young adults; and the shift in the saving function in response to declining relative capital-goods prices induced, once again, by unbalanced technological advance, this time favoring capital goods sectors. (Parenthetically, this outward shift in the saving function is generated for the following reasons: in equilibrium, r, the net rental rate on capital equals the product of the relative price of capital goods, P, and i, the interest rate or return to equity. To maintain short-run equilibrium, interest rates must rise at a rate equal to the percentage by which relative capital goods prices decline. At the same rental rate on capital, we would observe more saving as the relative price of capital goods declines.) Third, successful accumulation should, by diminishing returns, drive down the net rate of return over the century, thus cutting back the saving ratio from F to E.

It should be noted, incidentally, that the outward shift in the savings schedule cannot be defended by an appeal to some surge in nineteenth century capital inflows from abroad. Except for some brief critical episodes in the first half of the nineteenth century, foreign investment was always a small share of total domestic investment in America. More to the point, however, the foreign investment share in GNP declined over time, partly in response to the decline in the domestic rate of return to capital, and partly in response to America's increased ability to finance its accumulation requirements.

We are now equipped to decompose the sources of the rising nineteenth-century saving rates depicted in figure 3.1. We have the data describing equilibrium in the 1830s and the turn of the century, at A and E. Based on Lecture One, we also know by how much inequality rose over the same period, and by invoking the classical saving postulate – wage earners do not save – then we can place an upper bound on the shift in the saving function induced by rising inequality. All that remains is information on the saving and investment elasticities with respect to the rate of return. It can be shown that the elasticity of the long-run investment demand function is conditioned by the elasticity of substitution in some CES production function (but of opposite sign), and, therefore, we shall restrict our attention to cases where the elasticity lies between zero and minus one. Late nineteenth-century studies on the savings elasticity suggest that we restrict our attention here also to elasticities ranging between zero and one, although we will explore other more extreme cases as well.

I favor Case 1A in table 3.3. Under those "pessimistic" elasticity assumptions, the maximum impact of rising inequality on rising saving rates is modest, only one-fifth of the total increase. In contrast, the rise in investment demand – induced by the surge in labor-saving technical progress and labor-force growth – accounted for more than half the observed rise in net saving rates. The technology-induced decline in the relative price of capital goods accounted for almost a third. In short, the experiment suggests that the vast majority of rising saving rates in nineteenth-century America were technology or labor-force induced, while offering only the weakest support for the growth-equity trade-off, certainly much too weak to warrant the attention lavished on it in the historical and development literature. Note that the portion attributable to what I call exogenous saving mobilization (and/or the dependency effect) is trivial and negative. Does that result seem implausible? Not when we recall that the foreign investment share fell over the nineteenth century. Thus, the negative residual in Case 1A may simply reflect the drift towards self-financing over the century.

How robust are these results? Cases 1B through 1D offer some alternatives assuming different elasticities. In no case does the (upper bound) impact of rising inequality on saving rates exceed one-quarter of the total increase in saving rates across the century. The last two columns of table 3.3 offer two, more extreme, cases. Case 2 allows the saving function to be completely inelastic with respect to the net rate of return. I view this case as grossly unrealistic, but even here rising inequality can explain only about 40 percent of the increase in net saving ratios. Case 3 assumes a perfectly elastic saving function with respect to the net rate of return. Here, of course, distribution has no impact at all.

The historical morals seem to me well worth stressing. The time series evidence from nineteenth-century America confirms a high positive correlation between inequality, capital formation shares, and accumulation performance. The correlation is certainly close enough to have suggested support for the classic view of capitalist development where growth and equity are in conflict. Indeed, the conflict was sufficiently obvious to nineteenth-century economists that their models

Table 3.3 Decomposing the Sources of Rising American Nineteenth-century Net Investment Rates: The Long View

	Case 1A $\epsilon = -0.5$ $\eta = 1.0$	Case 1B $\epsilon = -0.3$ $\eta = 1.0$	Case 1C $\epsilon = -0.7$ $\eta = 1.0$	Case 1D $\epsilon = -0.5$ $\eta = 0.5$	Case 2 $\epsilon = -0.5$ $\eta = 0$	Case 3 $\epsilon = -0.5$ $\eta = \infty$
Total increase in net saving ratio	0.0700	0.0700	0.0700	0.0700	0.0700	0.0700
1 Technology and labor-force induced	0.0718	0.0708	0.0828	0.0676	0.0471	0.0762
Investment demand impact (B–A)	0.0368	0.0470	0.0359	0.0276	0	0.0552
Distribution impact (C–B)	0.0146	0.0110	0.0179	0.0202	0.0300	0
Decline in capital goods prices impact (D–C)	0.0204	0.0128	0.0290	0.0198	0.0171	0.0210
2 Residual mobilization impact (E–D)	−0.0018	−0.0008	−0.0128	0.0024	0.0229	−0.0062

Source: Williamson (1979, Table 3, p. 246)

of development were all built on the premise that accumulation rates could only be increased by shifts in income toward property-income recipients. A revisionist literature has accumulated since then, however, which tends to deflate the influence of distribution on saving performance. Yet, even the oft-cited work of William Cline (1972), Alan Blinder (1980), and others fails to offer a true alternative to the classical model since they only confront the impact of inequality on saving, ignoring the explanation of inequality itself. The advantage of the classical model is that distribution and accumulation are both endogenous variables. Perhaps this explains why the Ricardian–Marxian systems are just as central to modern growth and distribution theory today as they were a century ago. The theoretical tradition is alive, of that there is no doubt, and it is in large part based on correlations like those uncovered by American growth, inequality, and accumulation experience. It looks, however, like the correlation is spurious.

3 What about Britain? Does the First Industrial Revolution Confirm the Smithian Trade-off?

American nineteenth-century growth experience does not seem to offer much support for some Smithian trade-off between accumulation and equality. But perhaps American experience was unique. Perhaps we would find historical support for the trade-off view in other industrial revolutions. Indeed, what about the First Industrial Revolution? After all, it was British experience with early industrialization which motivated the classical model in the first place, and inequality is the critical force driving savings and accumulation in such models.

The piece of evidence which encouraged the classical economists to think in trade-off terms was stable real wages. That is, how was it possible for rapid industrialization to occur while at the same time the standard of living of the working classes changed so little? Marx tried to explain that fact by appealing to technological forces. Labor-saving technological change in industry and enclosures pushing labor off the land in agriculture both served to augment the reserve army, keeping the lid on unskilled labor's real wage. Although Malthus appears to have been unaware that an industrial revolution was taking place around him, his model could explain these events by appealing to a demographic response. Any improvement in real wages in the short run served to foster early marriage, greater fertility within marriage, as well as an elastic immigration response from Ireland, thus driving down the real wage in the longer run. Others appealed to disguised unemployment in the Irish and English countryside which ensured an elastic labor supply, and, as a result, no real-wage increase. In these classical models of stable real wages, rising inequality fosters rapid accumulation, but there is an absence of capital deepening since any increase in the capital stock will induce an equal increase in employment along an elastic labor supply function.

In contrast, Ricardo seems to have appealed to capital-scarcity and *slow* industrialization to get stable wages and labor surplus. In the Ricardian model, the causation seems to go from slow capital-deepening to labor surplus. Given the inelastic supply of land, rents increase their share in national income, a savings shortfall results from landlords' lack of thrift, and accumulation slows down. As capital-deepening comes to a halt, labor's marginal product stabilizes at subsistence wages.

As the British economy passed through a "turning point" in the middle of the nineteenth century (to coin a phrase used by John Fei and Gus Ranis), and real wages began to rise markedly, British economists lost interest in these classical growth paradigms. Instead, they went the more optimistic neoclassical route, and it became the dominant interpretation of economic growth for almost a century. But as Third World development attracted economists' attention in the 1950s, Arthur Lewis asked us to take another look at those discarded classical models. The implication was that the Third World in the 1950s closely resembled Britain in the late eighteenth and early nineteenth century. If the classical models worked well then, they should work well for the contemporary Third World too, and Lewis's celebrated labor surplus model emerged as a result.

The point of this recitation is simply to remind us that the labor surplus model has its roots with the classical (non-Ricardian) economists, and that their paradigms were developed to account for the economic events they thought were taking place around them. Were they right? I suspect they were not (Williamson, 1985b).

Were Real Wages Stable?

Were real wages stable during the British industrial revolution? Debate over this question is as old as the revolution itself. Thanks to the computer, archival collaboration, and liberal research funding, we now know far more about what happened to real wages during the First Industrial Revolution than did the classical economists or historians like Max Hartwell and Eric Hobsbawm who debated the issue in the 1950s and 1960s. The answer turns out to hinge on which side of 1820 we look. Figure 3.2 shows clearly that real wages were indeed stable up to about 1820. It also shows that unskilled common labor lagged behind when the real wages of the more skilled workers began to exhibit dramatic growth after 1820 (farm labor and urban unskilled – the "middle group" – enjoying much slower improvements in living standards). As Lecture One argued, income inequality rose across the century following 1760 as well, tracing out the familiar Kuznets Curve.

It appears that the classical economists were right after all. Real wages were stable up to 1820, and when real wages rise afterward, the unskilled wage lags far behind.

Was the British Industrial Revolution Really "Revolutionary"?

Were the classical economists also right in assuming that British industrialization was "revolutionary"? If they were wrong on this second point, then what we need are expla-

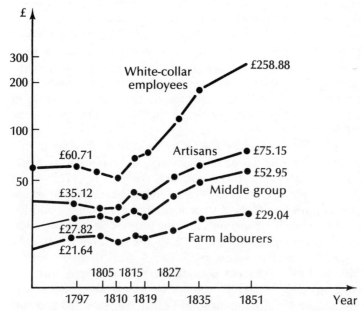

Figure 3.2 Average full-time earnings for adult male workers in Britain, 1797–1851, at constant prices.
Source: Williamson (1985a, p. 18)

nations of slow growth, not labor surplus models of rapid growth with stable real wages. That is, we need more Ricardian thinking and less Malthusian and Marxian thinking on the early industrialization up to 1820.

New and revisionist evidence confirms that somewhere around 1820 Britain passed through a secular turning point. Growth in national income was much lower before than after: growth in per capita income was only about 0.3 percent per annum from 1770 to 1815 while about 0.9 percent from 1815 to 1841. The growth rate doubling or tripling is apparent in the indexes of industrial production too, and, as we have seen, the turning point is equally dramatic for real wages. British growth before the 1820s, then, was modest at best. By the standards of the many industrial revolutions to follow, Britain's per capita income growth before 1820 is hardly impressive. In the two or three decades before World War One, Meiji Japan recorded a performance five times that, and America did the same in the middle of the nineteenth century. Even during the uneven 1970s, the developing countries managed an average per capita income growth rate of 3.2 percent per year, ten times the British rate before the 1820s.

British growth before the 1820s looks odd when set beside the conventional dating of the industrial revolution. Consistent with the labor surplus model, there is no evidence of improvement in the standard of living among the working classes until the 1820s. But inconsistent with the labor surplus model, growth of income and the rate of industrialization were both surprisingly slow. Furthermore, table 3.4 (col. 8) shows that Britain was a low saver. A gross domestic saving rate of 9 or 10 percent is certainly low compared with the contemporary developing country average of about 20 percent in 1977, or Meiji Japan around World War One (28 percent, 1910–16), or post-bellum America (23 percent, 1869–78). In addition, the saving rate only rises from 9 to 13 percent up to 1820, hardly the dramatic increase predicted by the labor surplus model, and certainly well below the 5 to 15 percent increase in the net saving rate thought by Arthur Lewis to characterize the "central problem in the theory of development." In fact, the rate of accumulation was very modest. Between 1760 and 1830 – the "heroic" age of the First Industrial Revolution – the rate of capital stock growth was only 1.2 percent per annum. Since the labor force grew at only 1 percent per annum, the capital–labor ratio drifted upward at the very leisurely pace of 0.2 percent per annum, far below the American rate of capital-deepening during the ante-bellum period (1.6 percent). The First Industrial Revolution looks very odd indeed, and it does not seem to support the labor surplus model very well. In spite of stable real wages, the saving rate remained low and the rate of accumulation was very modest.

Table 3.4 Public Debt Issues, Gross Domestic Saving in Reproducible Capital, and Gross Private Savings: Levels and Shares in National Income, England, 1761–1821

Year	Nominal Government Debt Outstanding (£ million) D (1)	National Income Price Deflator (1851–61 = 1.0) P_y (2)	Real Debt Outstanding D/P_y (3)	Decade	Increase per year in government debt			Shares in real national income %		
					P_y (4)	Nominal D (5)	Real D/P_y (6)	Debt Increase D/P_y (7)	Savings and Investment S/P_1 (8)	Gross Private Saving Rate (%) $S/P_1 + D/P_y$ (9)
1761	103.2	0.77	134.7							
1771	130.2	0.90	144.9	1761–71	0.83	2.7	3.3	3.6	9.1	12.7
1781	173.7	0.95	183.2	1771–81	0.92	4.4	4.7	4.9	10.5	15.4
1791	243.6	1.00	244.9	1781–91	0.97	7.0	7.2	6.5	13.3	19.8
1801	443.1	1.50	295.6	1791–1801	1.25	20.0	16.0	11.5	13.5	24.9
1811	618.9	1.60	387.3	1801–11	1.55	17.6	11.4	6.6	9.0	15.6
1821	838.0	1.19	703.6	1811–21	1.40	21.9	15.7	7.4	13.0	20.4

Source: Williamson (1984, Table 1, p. 176)

Why was the saving rate and the rate of accumulation so low during a period of high and rising inequality? One answer might be that Britain tried to do two things at once – industrialize *and* fight expensive wars, and she simply did not have the resources to do both (Williamson, 1984). During the 60 years following 1760, Britain was at war for 36; in the three decades following the late 1780s Britain went from a peacetime economy to a level of wartime commitment that had no parallel until World War One. The war mobilized a good share of the labor force, sugesting that the civilian economy faced labor scarcity. The war debt grew rapidly, suggesting that civilian capital accumulation was suppressed by crowding out. Tax revenues surged to one-fifth of national income, implying that real private incomes after tax were eroded. Meanwhile, war, blockades, and embargoes diminished international trade, inflating the relative prices of agricultural and raw material importables in the home market while lowering the price of manufactured exportables deflected from world markets.

Could the modest rate of accumulation have been the result of limited saving, constrained by war? That is the way many contemporary observers saw it, and it sounds like Ricardian capital-scarcity. Indeed, John Stuart Mill had an anti-Barro view of crowding out in which new war debt issues displaced private capital accumulation, one-for-one. A century later, T. S. Ashton (1955, 1959) affirmed the crowding-out hypothesis, whose main victims were building and construction, or what we would call today social overhead.

The first step in testing the Mill–Ashton hypothesis is to compute the size of the war debt. Table 3.4 shows that it was vast: the average burden of net additions to the war debt was 8.5 percent of national income between 1791 and 1821. The second step is to get an estimate of the gross private saving rate, that is, new public war debt should be added to civilian reproducible capital formation. When it is, Britain's private saving rates no longer seem so modest. Indeed, while table 3.4 shows that domestic investment in reproducible capital averaged only 11.4 percent of national income from 1761 to

1820, the gross private saving rate averaged 18.1 percent. Furthermore, while the investment share only rose from 9.1 to 13 percent in the six decades following the 1760s, the gross private saving rate rose from 12.7 to 20.4 percent, an increase more in tune with Arthur Lewis's dictum. It appears that Britain wasn't a modest saver early in the First Industrial Revolution after all. What makes Britain unusual is that much of the potential saving went into financing war.

Accumulation, Inequality, and the Labor Surplus Model

The labor surplus model confronts Lewis's "central problem" of development theory – understanding why net saving rates rise from something like 5 to 15 percent of national income during industrial revolutions – by adopting the classical trade-off view of inequality and accumulation. Stable real wages imply greater inequality, and inequality breeds higher saving rates, a surge in accumulation, and thus the industrial revolution.

The British historical evidence has not been kind to the labor surplus model. Although the real wage was certainly stable up to 1820, the investment rate only rose by about 4 percentage points between the 1760s and about 1820. And while inequality was sharply on the rise after 1820 as Britain passed through the upswing of the Kuznets Curve, the investment share failed to rise at all up to the 1850s. The lack of correlation between inequality and accumulation does not bode well for the labor surplus model, or the classical trade-off thinking upon which it is based.

For the period prior to 1820, I have offered an alternative explanation consistent with the simultaneous appearance of the low investment rates, the slow rates of accumulation, the lack of capital-deepening, and, of course, stable real wages. The explanation lies with war and its impact on the civilian economy. Although I do not have the space to offer the full argument and evidence, it can be shown that a computable general equilibrium model which captures the impact of war debt crowding out, labor mobilization, and food scarcity due to trade deflection can adequately account for all the peculiarities of the British industrial revolution up to 1820 (Williamson, 1984, 1985a, 1985b). To repeat, a classical model of labor surplus and Smithian trade-off is not required to explain stable real wages and rising inequality early in Britain's industrial revolution. A neoclassical model with Ricardian overtones can do better.

The period after the French wars also fails to support the labor surplus model. The critical evidence, of course, is that the real wage begins a significant rise after 1820. Stable real wages were simply not a characteristic of the British industrial revolution during those four decades of dramatic industrialization up to the 1850s. Inequality *was* on the rise, however, and much of it was attributable to the fact that unskilled wages lagged behind. But if inequality was on the rise, why does the investment share in national product show no rise after 1820? We may not have very good explanations for this puzzle, but it is clear that the rise in inequality did not induce a rise in the investment share. The Smithian trade-off fails for precisely the period for which it was first designed.

4 Have We Been Asking the Wrong Question All Along?

The evidence from two important industrial revolutions in the past seems to be inconsistent with the Smithian trade-off hypothesis: rising inequality was not a critical determinant of rising rates of conventional capital accumulation in nineteenth-century Britain and America. But what about human capital accumulation? Sad to say, here economic historians have much less to offer.

One can well see why. First of all, the mode of accumulation in the nineteenth century appears to have been much more heavily directed towards conventional capital formation, while the mode of accumulation in the twentieth century seems to have been much more heavily directed towards human capital accumulation. This is certainly reflected in the kinds of growth models which the classical economists debated – ones in which land, labor, and conventional capital were the key inputs, where investment in machines was a key source of growth, and where rent, profits, and wages were the distributional variables that mattered. As the twentieth century unfolded, this way of thinking was found increasingly inadequate so that human capital was added as a critical input, investment in human capital helped improve our understanding of the sources of growth, and the distribution of earnings became central to our thinking about inequality changes over time. Second, the problem is tougher. In contrast with conventional capital, and to state the obvious, human capital must be embodied in an individual, and imperfect capital markets make it difficult for those who *do* have the savings to invest in the human capital of those who do not. If rising inequality implies income constraints on the ability of the poor to invest in themselves, and if greater equality implies a partial release of that constraint, the Smithian trade-off is even more likely to be soundly rejected. But how important have these connections been historically? We do not know. Economic historians simply haven't asked the question in a coherent and systematic way.

That there has been a revolutionary increase in human-capital deepening over the past century or so is well known, at least as it is reflected in formal schooling. We see it in enrollment rates (an investment flow per capita) and we see it in schooling achievement (a stock per capita). Paul Schultz (1987) recently documented the revolutionary magnitude of this schooling experience between 1960 and 1980, and I reproduce it here in table 3.5. The rise in the schooling indicators there has been truly spectacular. Even more striking is the fact that the percentage gains in schooling were greatest among the poor countries who had the lower educational levels in 1960. The gap between rich and poor countries in what Schultz calls the "expected years of schooling" collapsed dramatically over those two decades. While such evidence might suggest to some that this catching up by the poor countries is a recent phenomenon, Richard Easterlin (1981) has shown that it has a much longer history. The sharp rise in enrollment rates in much of the Third World can be dated back at least to 1920, and in a few cases even to the late nineteenth century. Furthermore, figure 3.3 suggests that these Third World countries were also closing the gap with America and the European leaders long before 1960. What makes the 1960–80 period especially striking is how many poor countries had joined the catching-up club.

While there is evidence that the poor countries have been catching up to the rich in schooling investment rates, there is considerable variance in performance nonetheless. In the nineteenth century, America and Germany had far higher educational commitments than did France and the United Kingdom, suggesting quite different education accumulation regimes. Why was there so much variance even among the leading nineteenth-century industrializers? And the same question can be asked of the past two decades of Third World experience. Why is it that investment in schooling has been so low in Latin America and so high in East Asia, patterns that clearly emerge in the residuals from Schultz's model (1987, p. 447)?

One omitted variable might well be inequality. After all, incomes are far more equally distributed among the virtuous Asians. This can be seen clearly in table 3.6 (Williamson, 1989b) where the Kuznets Curve is reintroduced from Lecture One. Thus, the coefficient on the dummy variable Asia indicates that the eleven Asian countries in the sample (Hong Kong, Indonesia, Pakistan, Sri Lanka, India, Thailand, the Philippines, Korea, Taiwan, Malaysia and Japan) are significantly more egalitarian than the rest, and the differences are big. More or less the same results are forthcoming when only the Asian Pacific Rim countries are included (dummy variable Pacific Rim). When only Japan, Taiwan, and Korea are included (dummy variable Big 3), the results are even more striking: on average, the top 20 percent claimed 12 percent less of total income compared with other countries at comparable stages of development.

These differences warrant explanations, and we also need to know more about what contribution, if any, these more

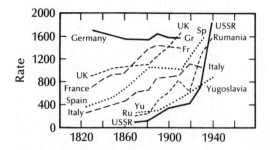

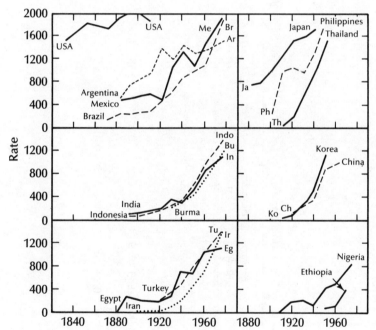

Figure 3.3 Primary school enrollment rates, 1830–1975 (per 10,000 population).

Source: Easterlin (1981, Figure 1, p. 8)

Table 3.5 Growth in Educational Enrollments by School Level and Countries by Income Class, 1960–1981

World Bank Country Class (number)	Primary (6–11) Education		Secondary (12–17) Education		Higher (20–24) Education		Expected Years of Schooling		Percentage Increase in Enrollment Ratios (1960–81)			
	1960	1981	1960	1981	1960	1981	1960	1981	Primary	Secondary	Higher	Expected
	(1)	(2)	(3)	(4)	(5)	(6)	(7)	(8)	(9)	(10)	(11)	(12)
Low Income (34)	0.80	0.94	0.18	0.34	0.02	0.04	5.98	7.88	18	89	100	32
Excluding China and India	0.38	0.72	0.07	0.19	0.01	0.02	2.75	5.56	89	171	100	102

Middle Income (38)

Oil exporters	0.64	1.06	0.09	0.37	0.02	0.08	4.48	8.98	66	311	300	100
Oil importers	0.84	0.99	0.18	0.44	0.04	0.13	6.32	9.23	18	144	225	46
Upper-Middle Income (22)	0.88	1.04	0.20	0.51	0.04	0.14	6.68	10.0	18	155	250	50
High-Income Oil exporters (5)	0.29	0.83	0.05	0.43	0.01	0.08	2.09	7.96	186	760	700	281
Industrial Market (18)	1.14	1.01	0.64	0.90	0.16	0.37	11.5	13.3	−11	41	131	16
East European Nonmarket (8)	1.01	1.05	0.45	0.88	0.11	0.20	9.31	12.6	4	96	82	35

Source: Schultz (1987, Table 1, p. 417)

Table 3.6 The Kuznets Curve and the Virtuous Asians

Variable	Dependent Variable							
	Share of Bottom 20%				Share of Top 20%			
	[1]	[2]	[3]	[4]	[5]	[6]	[7]	[8]
Constant	26.16	23.81	26.90	28.78	−51.66	−39.69	−54.64	−62.26
	(4.32)	(4.30)	(4.62)	(4.95)	(1.84)	(1.47)	(2.00)	(2.23)
ln (GNP/Pop)	−6.95	−6.35	−7.26	−7.67	36.96	33.92	38.22	40.55
	(3.60)	(3.39)	(3.91)	(4.21)	(4.14)	(3.96)	(4.39)	(4.89)
[ln (GNP/Pop)]^2	0.54	0.50	0.57	0.60	−3.13	−2.93	−3.24	−3.41
	(3.61)	(3.46)	(3.93)	(4.22)	(4.52)	(4.43)	(4.79)	(5.30)
Dummy: Asia		1.15				−5.90		
		(2.35)				(2.60)		
Dummy: Pacific Rim			1.29				−5.17	
			(2.35)				(2.02)	
Dummy: Big 3				2.45				−12.27
				(2.95)				(3.24)
$\bar{R}^2$	0.17	0.23	0.23	0.27	0.39	0.45	0.43	0.49
DW	1.64	1.62	1.64	1.68	2.03	2.11	2.12	2.25
F-stat	6.52	6.52	6.56	7.88	18.80	16.15	14.65	18.28

Figures in parentheses are t-statistics. Big 3 = Japan, Taiwan, and Korea; Pacific Rim = Big 3 plus Thailand, the Philippines, Malaysia, Hong Kong, and Indonesia; Asia = Pacific Rim plus Pakistan, Sri Lanka, and India.
Source: Williamson (1989b, Table 6)

egalitarian distributions have made to the more impressive commitment to education in East Asia, as well as the reverse in Latin America. While I am unaware of any quantitative analysis offering an explicit test, there is no shortage of hypotheses that might plausibly account for egalitarian East Asia (Williamson, 1989b). First, there is convenient historical accident: Japan, Korea, and Taiwan were all forced to introduce fundamental land reforms in the late 1940s and early 1950s, unique conditions which virtually eliminated farm tenancy. Not only was land redistributed, raising incomes of the poor at the bottom of the distribution, but those with middle incomes did not have to pay much for the redistribution through taxes since the value of government bonds used to compensate the landlords at the top of the distribution were eroded away by rapid inflation. Another convenient historical force was at work to redistribute wealth and income in these three economies – the destruction of wealth by war and inflation. Between 1935 and 1955, the wealth–income ratio in Japan declined precipitously from 4.15 to 2.20. This massive decline in the wealth–income ratio tended to equalize incomes (and subsequently to stimulate the saving rate) since the rich held most of the physical and financial assets destroyed. While I do not have similar evidence for Taiwan and Korea, the same forces may well have been at work there too. None of these forces were at work in Latin America, the more inegalitarian part of the Third World. In addition, there is the matter of comparative advantage and agricultural technologies. Rice culture is small-scale, encouraging family farms, labor-intensive technology, and more egalitarian ownership. Sugar cane, coffee, and other export crops typical of nineteenth- and twentieth-century Latin America are large-scale, encouraging commercial farms, inegalitarian ownership, and what Marx and British economic historians call a proletarianized agricultural labor market. This early specialization in different agricultural technologies is likely to have launched East Asia and Latin America on two quite different development paths. Surely these facts of history made it easier for the poor in Asia to invest in human capital than was true of their counterparts in Latin America or even in eighteenth-century Britain. And surely these facts of history were translated into more interventionist government policies which favored mass education in East Asia while suppressing it in Latin America and eighteenth-century Britain.

If this argument seems plausible, then I should see a negative correlation between inequality and commitment to educational investment. That is, I should be able to find historical evidence that rejects the Smithian trade-off even more soundly when investment is augmented to include human capital. Unfortunately, history tends to be unkind to simple mono-causal theories like this one. Figure 3.4 tells us why. Suppose income and earnings inequality are highly correlated, a proposition which has been confirmed by the economic histories of both Britain and the USA. Thus, we can put both skill scarcity and inequality on the vertical axis, although different economies with the same earnings inequality may have different income inequality due to the initial distribution of land and other factors. Along the horizontal axis we have skill saving and investment, like school enrollment rates. Let some industrial revolutionary event create a boom in skill investment demand, written here as a shift to I'. Left solely to private-sector responses, one economy with more inequality and lower incomes for the poor might exhibit an inelastic response to the skill scarcity starting at A and ending up at D. Another more egalitarian economy is likely to find its poor better able to respond to skill scarcity ending up at B. This more egalitarian economy is also likely to set in motion political forces to increase the commitment to public education, perhaps shifting the skill investment supply function to the right, generating a new equilibrium at C. Were that all there was to the story, we would have the raw historical correlation we are looking for, equality associated with high investment in skills and a rejection of the trade-off. However, there is no reason to expect that all countries will be faced with the same demand forces. Suppose the more egalitarian economy pursues a more unskilled labor intensive growth regime so that the boom in skill investment demand is muted, say to I″. The new equilibrium for the more egalitarian economy is now at C″. What will history now reveal? No correlation at all between inequality and investment in skills since D and C″ imply the same commitment to human capital accumulation.

Can we unravel the influence of growth regime from skill-supply response when assessing the trade-off? Which has dominated in the past? Nineteenth-century Britain clearly looks like the inequality-regime scenario which moves along the path from A to D, much like contemporary Brazil, while East Asia looks more like the egalitarian-regime scenario which moves along the path from A to C or C″. But we need more evidence, and for this I turn once more to Paul Schultz's paper.

Schultz (1987) develops a production-demand model to explain the variance in commitment to education among countries between 1960 and 1980, where incomes, prices, educational production technology, and demographic variables all play their conventional roles. What is missing from the model, however, is an explicit statement of the market forces generating different investment demand for education, or of the income distributional forces influencing educational supply responses. I have been able to add the latter to his model, but, alas, not the former (Williamson, 1989b). Table 3.7 presents the results for a somewhat smaller sample than Schultz's, since income distributional evidence is available for fewer countries. Only two dependent variables (all in logs) are reported in the table: the enrollment ratio and expenditure per school-aged child. Furthermore, the analysis is limited to secondary education where the variance across countries is greatest. The explanatory variables include four of Schultz's – income, the relative price of teachers, percent urban, and the share of the population of secondary school age – and our added distributional variable. The estimated parameters on Schultz's variables more or less reproduce his results: educational commitment rises with income; where the relative price of teachers is high (that is, where capital goods are expensive), fewer children are educated (the enrollment rates are low), even though expenditure rates are swollen; a Malthusian glut of school-aged children crowds children out of the schools and lowers the expenditure commitment per enrolled child as capital-widening diverts resources from capital-deepening; and urbanization has no significant influence. Income distribution has the predicted effect: more egalitarian societies (where the bottom 40 percent have high income shares relative to the top 20 percent) make a greater commitment to education, but the correlation is weak. There is no evidence here which supports the Smithian trade-off, but there is also only weak evidence which confirms the contrary view. I suspect the reason for those small t-statistics on the income distribution variable can be found in figure 3.4: societies with high inequality also pursue growth regimes that generate big booms in skill investment demand like that at I', while the opposite is true of more egalitarian societies. I have not been able to prove that assertion, and it certainly has high research priority.

5 The Bottom Line

I have come to the end of the first three Kuznets Memorial Lectures. What does history tell us about inequality and modern economic growth?

A clearer understanding of the Kuznets Curve in the past has emerged. While the underlying theory claims no firm law, it does suggest those conditions under which inequality is likely to trace out a Kuznets Curve. As we have seen, these conditions need not hold for all nations undergoing modern economic growth, but they appear to have held for two important industrial revolutions, that of America and Britain.

Over the long sweep of Anglo-American growth from the early nineteenth century, the three prime movers of income inequality were: the rise and fall of unbalanced sectoral productivity growth, favoring capital and skill-intensive sectors early in the industrial revolution on the upswing of the Kuznets Curve, unskilled labor-saving forces which dissipate late

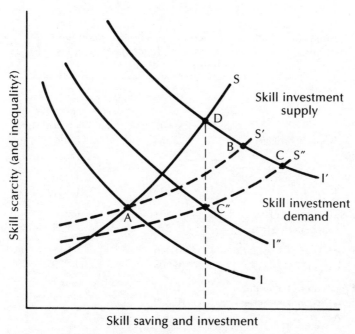

Figure 3.4 Skill investment demand and supply: the uncertain role of inequality.

in the industrial revolution on the downside of the Kuznets Curve; the rise and fall of labor force growth, forces of the demographic transition that were strongly reinforced by foreign immigration patterns; and the lagged acceleration in skills deepening. Magnitudes matter, and these forces may not be strong enough in some historic cases (like Japan) to outweigh the effects of human capital accumulation or the tendency of Engel's Law to undercut rural landed wealth. In some cases, the weakness of these forces may be more effective in explaining the absence of a rise in income inequality or a delay in the expected income leveling.

History also suggests that an old lesson dating back to Adam Smith should be unlearned. American history suggests

Table 3.7 Estimates of Secondary School Expenditures and
Components, with the Price of Teachers Exogenous: 35
Countries, 1960–80

Explanatory Variable	Dependent Variable in Logarithms	
	Enrollment Ratio	Total Expenditure per Secondary School Aged Child
GNP per Adult in 1970 (log)	0.313 (2.379)	1.330 (10.931)
Relative Price of Teachers (log)	−0.457 (5.272)	0.629 (7.839)
Proportion of Population Urban	0.346 (0.608)	0.644 (1.222)
Proportion of Population of Secondary School Age	−1.860 (0.809)	−6.261 (2.944)
National Household Income Distribution (Bottom 40%/Top 20%)	0.796 (1.234)	0.956 (1.603)
Intercept	−3.045 (4.410)	−5.638 (8.820)
R^2	0.831	0.956
Sample Size	35	35

Relative price of teachers is treated as exogenous and estimated with ordinary least squares. Absolute value of t-ratio is reported in parentheses beneath regression coefficients.
Source: Williamson (1989b, Table 10)

that more inequality did not raise conventional accumulation by much. British history suggests that more inequality did not raise conventional accumulation at all. When human capital is added to the accumulation story, the Smithian trade-off receives an even sounder rejection by history.

4

Lecture Four
Poverty, Policy, and
Industrialization

1 Thinking about Poverty and Industrialization

Does industrialization and modern economic growth diminish poverty? On the face of it, the answer seems obvious. If by growth we mean an increase in per capita income, *and if there is no change in the distribution of that income*, then by definition the incomes of the poor will rise along with everything else, and the rate of escape from poverty will exhibit the same performance. This "trickle down" theorem suggests that it is not possible to discuss the relation between growth and poverty without discussing its effect on distribution, as indeed we have seen in the previous three lectures. Has the rise in inequality been so severe in the past that the percentage in poverty could have risen and the average living standards among the poor diminished? Such results would have required severe inequality trends indeed, but it is important to understand that the forces driving inequality are similar to the forces driving poverty. While rising inequality may not necessarily imply increasing poverty, it may imply a slow rate of escape from poverty.

Modern economic growth can affect poverty in both direct and indirect ways. The direct influence has already been stated: if incomes of the poor rise along with the average, then poverty can be said to have diminished. The indirect influence takes account of the fact that much of the poverty which we observe in both the nineteenth century and today occurs at predictable stages in an individual's life cycle. The incidence of poverty is greatest among those who are not full income earners like the aged, or among those subject to crisis like the sick or widowed. It is a mistake to infer that higher incomes have no indirect impact on such individuals who are cut off from the market economy. After all, those who receive higher incomes should be better able to save more for crises and old age, including the working poor. And the growth and wider access of financial institutions for saving, credit, and insurance should help even poor individuals spread their lifetime incomes over their lifetime needs. Furthermore, a richer society might be expected to be willing and able to transfer more resources to those in need whether by state intervention, by private charity, or by intra-family transfers. As it turns out, however, none of these indirect potential connections between higher incomes and poverty helped the poor very much in the nineteenth century.

There are four ways that the share in poverty might fail to fall during early industrial revolutions. First, and as we have seen, the earnings of the poor may lag behind in response to technological events driving industrial revolutions. Second, the cost of living facing the poor may rise more dramatically for exactly the same reasons, eroding their living standards in ways which conventional income statistics may fail to capture. Third, early industrial revolutions may undermine both the earning potential of secondary unskilled workers and the secondary earning sources of primary unskilled workers. Fourth, modern economic growth may erode traditional entitlements which serve as safety nets in pre-industrial societies. Let us dwell a moment on each of these.

The most important way that early industrialization might raise poverty, or at least inhibit its eradication, is if it generates rising inequality. Lecture One showed that there is a fair amount of evidence supporting a nineteenth-century upswing of a Kuznets Curve, at least in Britain and America. Furthermore, inequality seems to have been driven by technological forces which were unskilled labor saving, a view stressed by Marx and explored at length by development economists in the 1960s and 1970s. The derived demand for unskilled labor simply does not share equally in the boom for other primary inputs – like land, skills, and capital – during early industrial revolutions. And if the working poor suffer, those in extreme poverty will suffer even more.

There is a second, and directly related, way that early industrial revolutions can inhibit poverty eradication. Technical change during early industrial revolutions in the nineteenth century was slowest in those activities which produced goods and services which figured most prominently in the budgets of the poor. The two most important of these were food and urban housing. The terms of trade between farm and nonfarm goods rose across most of the nineteenth century, so that food became relatively expensive, driving up the cost of living of the poor relative to higher income classes for whom the food expenditure share was much smaller. The source of this long-run trend was not the Heckscher–Ohlin theorem, so popular in trade theory, but rather unbalanced productivity advance favoring nonfarm sectors combined with inelastic land supplies. Land scarcity and technological events mattered most. Furthermore, the relative cost of urban housing rose by even more. Rents soared, and the poor were most significantly affected since expenditure on even their blighted and modest housing were so much larger as a share of their family budgets than among the higher income classes. And high and rising rents encouraged the poor to search for ever-cheaper dwellings, encouraging them to crowd into lower-quality housing which augmented mortality, morbidity, and their ability to work. We do not measure such environmental deterioration very well, but it seems to have been manifested by a decline in nutritional status and physical well-being during the industrial revolution (Fogel, 1989). While the intra-urban transport revolution did gradually increase the distances over which people could travel to work, making it increasingly possible to escape the worst slums by moving to the more benign periphery, it did not keep pace with the pressure of urbanization. Thus, the poor tended to concentrate in the environmentally deprived central core of nineteenth-century cities rather than at the periphery as is true in Third World squatter settlements today. This plus government neglect of urban infrastructure served to heighten the notorious crowding and slum living of the early nineteenth-century urban poor, a quality of urban life even lower than that observed for the worst Third World cities. In short, the same forces that tend to cause the income of the working poor to lag behind during early industrial revolutions also tend to raise their relative cost of living – industrialization tends to cheapen the goods that the poor produce relative to the goods that the poor consume.

Before moving on to the other forces which may have contributed to slow progress with poverty eradication early in the industrial revolution, it is worth reiterating that beneath the working poor were the extreme poor who were represented disproportionately by the old, the sick, large families, and female-headed households. This lecture will, therefore, consider more generally how technical change affected the demand for old labor, child labor, and female labor. A definitive historical answer to this crucial question is not yet within our grasp, but a key component to the answer is clearly the fate of the cottage or domestic industries. These industries were and are very important to the economic status of the poor. Domestic industries were and are intensive in their use of female, child, and old labor and hence important income sources for vulnerable groups. They were often low skill and low strength, and they could be (and are) undertaken alongside child care in the home where the pace of production was self-regulated. These industries were often an important secondary income source for the family that took on extra importance during agricultural slack seasons, during periods of low market employment, and during periods of food crisis. The rise of the factory and the development of integrated commodity markets tended to eliminate these cottage industries.

That fact is much stressed by pessimists in the standard of living debate, and I shall dwell on it at length later in this lecture.

The other chief way in which early industrialization might create increased distress among the poor is if there is an erosion of traditional means of support and entitlements. Although modernization theorists stress different forces, most of them make much of the long lag between the destruction of traditional support systems and their replacement by modern transfer mechanisms (Sen, 1981): for example, the erosion of the village "moral economy" (Scott, 1976); the breakup of the extended family and the rise of "individualization" (MacFarlane, 1978); and the increased importance of migration generating "child default" on parental investment (Williamson, 1986a). Within these entitlement-erosion themes are a number of important claims. For example, and as we have seen, Lindert (1989) argues that significant transfer systems were not introduced in the NICs of the past until the twentieth century, partly in response to the fact that economic conditions of the poor began to catch up with the rest of the economy on the downside of the Kuznets Curve, thus increasing their political voice. Others argue the contrary, and that government intervention was extensive – although local – even in pre-industrial societies. This debate should tell us much about attitudes towards poverty and how their evolution might be expected in the Third World if they obey the same historical laws.

Having suggested the main ways in which early industrialization might inhibit poverty eradication, we return to a central theme of these lectures. It is not economic growth *per se* that is sometimes said to make the poor poorer, but rather the processes and policies that are associated with various growth regimes that matter. Having said as much, it becomes clear that the kind of arguments sometimes put forward by the optimists are simply not relevant to the claims put forward by the pessimists. For example, in a recent survey for the World Bank, Gary Fields (1989) compares changes in the poverty share between Third World countries exhibiting rapid growth and those exhibiting stagnation. He concludes that the poor did better during periods of rapid growth. Similarly, the Council of Economic Advisors "discovered" in 1964 that the share in poverty declined by more in periods of rapid American growth. But no one ever suggested that the poor do better when an economy is stagnating than when it is booming – *given the economic structure and policy environment*. Surely rapid growth is better than slow growth in eradicating poverty, *given the economic structure and policy environment*. Rather, the issue is how changes in that structure and policy environment can affect the poor.

This is an ambitious set of questions, and despite the attention which historians have paid to them since Britain started the First Industrial Revolution, history yields the answers only with great reluctance. Yet, a survey of what we do know may still help place contemporary Third World debate in perspective. This final lecture, therefore, reports what nineteenth-century experience can tell us about the poverty, policy, and industrialization connection (Polak and Williamson, 1989).

2 Trends in Poverty

A Word about the Evidence

What can we say about the extent and composition of poverty in the nineteenth-century industrializing countries? Irma Adelman and Cynthia Taft Morris (1978, 1988) have used a wide range of sources to compare poverty across countries in the nineteenth century. The evidence they collected in 1978 led them to pessimistic conclusions: "at low levels of development any kind of structural change such as industrialization or expanded commercialization tends to increase poverty among the poorest members of the population" (1978, p. 256). While they are much less pessimistic in their 1988 book, much of the evidence behind their assessment, however, is still qualitative and impressionistic. There are dangers in using such evidence. For example, an increase in writing about the poor in the nineteenth century need not reflect an increase in the extent of poverty. Upper classes may have been made more aware of poverty by changes in its location: rapid urbanization brought with it an increase in the most obvious and outward signs of poverty – residential crowding – located near the doorsteps of the urban middle classes. The impression that this squalor made on Henry Mayhew and Charles Dickens is important in its own right: it has shaped the popular image of poverty during the industrial revolution. Such evidence, however, will not easily support quantitative claims that there was more poverty in rapidly industrializing England than in slower industrializing France, where more of the poor were rural and out of sight. It may say more about awareness of poverty than its prevalence.

We need numbers. Ideally, we would like to have household survey data of the kind favored by Fields (1989, p. 5) in his recent survey of poverty and economic growth in the contemporary Third World. Unfortunately, no such data exist for most of the nineteenth century. It is only toward the end of the century that a series of detailed investigations of urban poverty were made that can claim to be the precursors of the kind of household surveys which Fields favors. For earlier periods, we have to rely on data generated by the provision of poor relief by local administrators to "paupers" in Britain and America. How good are such data in documenting trends in poverty?

Figure 4.1 tests the claim that pauper statistics can be used to proxy poverty. It uses a survey made at 28 places in England in 1899 of incomes of people over age 65. The horizontal axis shows the proportion of old people who had incomes under 10s a week among those whose incomes are known. The vertical axis shows the proportion of old people surveyed who were or had been on outside poor relief. There is a clear if imperfect relation between the numbers living on low incomes and those on poor relief. This relationship is even stronger when we control for policy (Polak and Williamson, 1989).

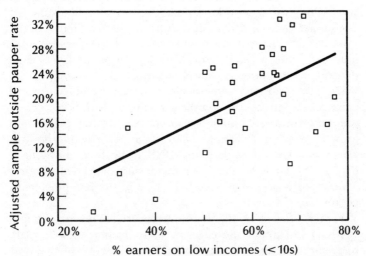

Figure 4.1 Old age poor and old age pauperism, England and Wales, 1899.
Source: Polak and Williamson (1989)

Does Economic Growth Reduce Poverty?

Having established that pauperism can be used as an imperfect proxy for poverty, what can we say about long-term trends? Figure 4.2 (from Williams, 1981, p. 164) shows long-run trends in the pauper rate for England, 1840–1939. At first sight, there appears to be a clear trend downward in the pauper rate from the late 1840s up to World War One. However, a closer look reveals that it is *outdoor* pauperism that declined. While some have concluded that the overall decline is evidence of the authorities' success in limiting access to outdoor relief rather than an improvement in the standard of living of the extreme poor, the decline in overall pauper rates after the 1840s *is*, nonetheless, consistent with the inequality and unskilled wage trends discussed in Lecture One. True, outdoor relief was systematically cut in the 1870s. However, the decline in figure 4.2 continues up to the eve of

World War One and surely that is explained largely by real wage gains for the working poor. It may also be explained by the accelerated decline in fertility after the 1880s. As the number of dependants declined, more single parents were able to get by without being driven into pauperism. These dependency rate effects should have played a symmetric role when poverty rates were rising in the late eighteenth and early nineteenth century on the upswing of the English demographic transition which yields peak rates of population growth between 1820 and 1840. That is, a good share of rising poverty up to 1820 or 1840 is likely to have been driven by rising fertility and increasing dependency rates. The opposite seems to have been true in the late nineteenth century.

Figure 4.2 deals with trends in poverty following the late 1840s. What about the early industrialization period, years of greater interest to contemporary analysis of Third World

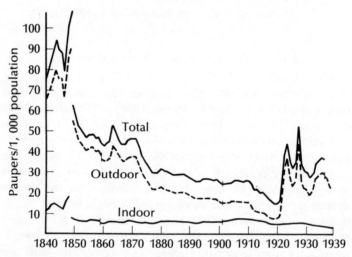

Figure 4.2 Paupers per 1,000 of population in England, 1840–1939.
Source: Williams (1981)

problems? Here we are on shakier ground. The original "social tables" by Gregory King, Joseph Massie, Patrick Colquhoun, and Dudley Baxter took very different approaches to estimating pauperism, but they did supply some well-informed guesses. The revised social tables imply the following trends for the percentage in poverty (Williamson, 1985a; p. 70): 1759, 12.5; 1801–3, 19.9; 1812, 14.8; 1850, 10.0; and 1867, 6.2. The shares in poverty rose in the late eighteenth century, a period of rising inequality and stable real wages of the poor. The rate of fall between 1812 and 1850 was slow, 0.3 percent per decade, while it accelerated thereafter, 2.2 percent, a result consistent with figure 4.2 and with the inequality and unskilled real wage trends documented in Lecture One. Of course, changes in the supply of relief may have influenced those estimates of poverty, relief generosity having risen up to the early nineteenth century, falling by 1850. While these trends must therefore be treated with caution, they do confirm that economic growth reduces poverty, but that the rate of poverty reduction can vary considerably.

Table 4.1 reports pauper rates for New York State at five-year intervals starting in 1835. Pauperism (and poverty) was on the rise throughout the ante-bellum period, and Hannon views these trends as evidence of an increase in the demand for poor relief and thus of the distress of the poor. The big gains in poverty reduction, according to such proxies, came after 1865 when American industrialization hits full stride, much like Britain.

Regional Variation in Poverty: Industrialization and Urbanization

We might get a better impression of the aggregate effect of long-term economic development on the poor by comparing pauper rates in agricultural with industrial counties. Table 4.2 offers exactly that kind of evidence for the early stages of the British industrial revolution, 1803–4. When London is excluded, the last two rows of the table suggest that there was no obvious difference in the generosity of relief policy

Table 4.1 Local Relief Recipients per 1,000 Population, New
York State, 1835–1895

Year	New York State	New York City	Rest of State
1835	18.69	84.03	8.73
1840	25.17	88.11	15.27
1846	38.51	146.43	18.93
1850	42.26	97.47	29.13
1855	65.04	160.61	39.73
1860	65.93	138.42	42.33
1865	81.10	233.98	39.95
1870	51.50	85.43	40.96
1874	68.49	130.68	47.77
1880	55.03	124.79	28.79
1885	39.84	86.72	22.42
1890	35.21	64.74	21.59
1895	35.07	54.03	26.96

There is no figure for 1845. The figures for 1875 are out of line
with the neighboring years. They are 101.43; 253.40; and 53.38
respectively.
Source: Hannon (1986, Appendix A, pp. 9–10)

(as measured by the proportion of paupers forced into the
workhouse) between agricultural and industrial counties.
However, despite the high agricultural prices at that time
caused by the Napoleonic War, a far higher proportion were
on relief in the agricultural counties. This suggests either that
poverty was more widespread in agricultural areas or that it
was more widespread in those areas (the south) most distant
from new industrial job opportunities (the north). What data
we do have suggests that the latter seems more likely. Of the
agricultural counties, the two northernmost listed (Lincoln
and Rutland) were the least pauperized. Among the ten industrial counties listed, three of the four with pauper rates over
13 percent are southern while five of the six with rates under
10 percent are northern.

Table 4.2 County Pauper Statistics, England and Wales, 1803–1804

Region	Total Paupers per Population (%)	Indoor/Total Paupers (%)
England and Wales	11.4	8.0
"Industrial Counties"	9.5	10.9
"Agricultural Counties"	16.1	7.7
"Industrial counties" excluding Middlesex and Surrey (i.e. London)	9.8	7.2

"Agricultural and Industrial" are as defined in the original *Parliamentary Papers*.
Source: Williams (1981, pp. 150–1)

It appears that in the midst of the British industrial revolution, the poor fared better in the *regions* that underwent industrialization. Indeed, the effect on poverty of higher incomes and greater earning opportunities generated by industrialization in the north spilled over into the agricultural areas within the region. The rural poor could and did move to urban areas, with the result that higher wages and less poverty prevailed everywhere in the north.

Who Were the Poor and Who Were the Paupers?

It is important to ask who were poor and who were paupers for two reasons. First, economic development may affect different groups in different ways. If we can identify the groups that are poor we may be able to say something more useful about the relation of poverty to growth. Second, there may be differences between the composition of the poor and that of the paupers. The poor were largely in households of low-wage, unskilled workers so the main forces driving changes in their well-being were those discussed in Lecture One. The paupers, on the other hand, represent the *extreme* poor. Their well-being may be less directly related to the wages of the unskilled.

Male able-bodied pauperism fell over the century in England: the number of male able-bodied paupers in 1901 was approximately 7 percent of the number relieved in this category a century earlier (Williams, 1981, pp. 40–1). Part of this fall was the result of a conscious effort by British authorities to refuse outdoor relief to healthy adult males. The other force was market related – rising wages driven by market forces already discussed.

By the end of the century, however, we must look beyond the adult male workforce when discussing pauperism and extreme poverty. Then, as now, the old, the sick, widows, children of single parents, and those in large families were much more likely to be very poor. Poverty obeys the life cycle. This is illustrated in figure 4.3 which shows pauper rates in England and Wales in March 1906 by age group. The solid line shows total pauper rates and the broken line indoor pauper rates. Pauper rates rise steeply in old age. Almost one in five of the population over 65 and almost one in four of those over 70 were receiving poor relief at the time of this census.

Those over 65 constituted 28.3 percent of all paupers in the 1906 census and 35.3 percent of those in the workhouses. Unfortunately, there are no data on the ages of outdoor paupers before 1890, but the percentage of paupers who were listed as "not able-bodied" (a category in which 80 percent were over age 60 in 1906) rises from 38.9 percent in 1850 to a peak of 49.2 percent in 1900. The percentage of indoor paupers over age 65 rose in the same period from 19.8 percent to 36.5 percent of the workhouse population (Williams, 1981, pp. 204–5). In both cases, part of the rise was due to the restriction of outdoor relief to the old that took place in the 1870s but the trends continue until 1900 suggesting that government policy is not the only driving force.

Three conclusions seem warranted by the data. First, the economic position of the elderly was falling behind that of the

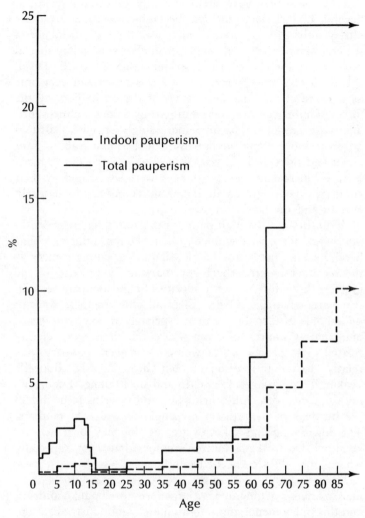

Figure 4.3 Life-cycle poverty, 1906 (indoor and total pauperism as a percentage of population in age group, England and Wales, March 1906).
Source: Williams (1981)

rest of the working class in the late nineteenth century. Second, English poor relief was becoming less generous to the old over the same period. In any case, the high incidence of poverty among the elderly suggests that we should pay special attention to the effects of industrialization on the old. Third, this older and more vulnerable age class increased over time as a share of total paupers, a result driven in part by the forces of industrialization, and in part by demographic events. The latter influence became increasingly strong as Britain began to move along the downside of the demographic transition and the elderly increased in relative importance. Similarly, an increasing number of aged were left behind by their children who migrated in increasing numbers to cities in Britain and the new world.

In addition to the high pauper rates in old age revealed in figure 4.3, there was a much smaller "hump" during childhood, peaking between 10 and 14 and then falling rapidly as the teenager entered the labor market. By the end of the nineteenth century only a minority of child paupers were in two parent families. Over half of all child paupers were in households headed by women, especially widows: the economic circumstances of women and children were closely related. The proportion of women who were paupers rises relative to the proportion of men through early adult life peaking between ages 35 and 45 and then falling. The upswing coincides with childbearing age and it seems to be due to the burdens of parenthood on single or widowed mothers. The downswing may reflect a greater tendency for women to be supported in their children's homes than men, especially where grandchildren needed minding.

The vulnerability of widows to pauperism should be familiar to anyone acquainted with modern developing countries, and this phenomenon did not originate with industrialization. What evidence we have for pre-industrial England suggests that it was far harder for a widow to remarry than a widower and especially hard if the widow had dependent children. Supporting a family as a single parent is difficult now, and it was then. Consequently, almost 40 percent of widow-headed households in eighteenth-century England were on relief. We have now looked at the composition of English pauperism. How about the composition of English poverty? Table 4.3 gives a breakdown of the proximate causes of urban poverty at the end of the century from the investigations of Booth, Rowntree, and Bowley. It is clear that most of the poverty was associated with low wages or large families. This, widow-headed households, the old, and the sick made up a far smaller proportion of the poor than of the extreme poor, that is, of paupers. And while most child pauperism was explained by single-earner families, most child poverty occurred in large families where the chief earner was low paid. In any case, the proximate causes of poverty in America were not very different from those for England (Hannon, 1986, p. 97).

Seasons, Cycles, and Secondary Activities

By secondary occupations, I mean jobs typically undertaken either by secondary earners in a household or by the prime earner as a secondary income source. What were these occupations? Before and during the early stages of industrialization, rural domestic, household, or cottage industries such as spinning and weaving often supplemented the household's main income source. Later in the industrial revolution, we see the development of what are called the "sweated" trades, like clothes-making shops, most notably in large cities like London and New York. Throughout we see those occupations that are now associated with the "informal sector" in the Third World like cleaning or street hawking.

Domestic manufacturing was hardly the only secondary occupation important in rural areas. Whether owner occupiers or tenants, small farmers often had a variety of land uses in addition to their major crop. Households whose main source of income was wage labor also cultivated a small plot on which they grew crops either for their own consumption or for the local market. Even landless households in pre-industrial England kept their own livestock, using the commons for

Table 4.3 Principal Immediate Causes of Poverty in Five English
Towns (% of Poor Households Below Rowntree Standard)

Immediate Cause	Northampton 1913	Warrington 1913	Bolton 1914	Reading 1913	York 1899
Chief wage earner:					
Dead	21	6	35	14	27
Ill or old	14	1	17	11	10
Unemployed	–	3	3	2	3
Irregularly employed	–	3	6	4	3
Chief wage earner regularly employed *but*					
Wages insufficient for 3 children					
Families of:					
3 children or less	21	22	20	33	
4 children or more	9	38	9	15	
					57
Wages sufficient for 3 children but 4 children or more in family	35	27	10	21	
Total	100	100	100	100	100

Sources: Bowley and Burnett-Hurst (1915, p. 408). Bowley and Hogg
(1925, p. 158)

grazing, while urban workers often kept pigs and chickens.
   Such activities were of special importance to the poor.
These secondary activities formed part of the "safety net"
against poverty. At times of crisis, the secondary occupation
became the primary income source. Secondary industries
often had a different seasonal cycle than primary occupations

and hence smoothed both demands on household labor and thus the household's income. Outlets for the products and services of secondary industries were often localized and hence were less subject to macroeconomic demand fluctuations. A variety of household income sources spread market and other risks. Furthermore, these activities typically employed a high proportion of old, child, and female labor – groups most vulnerable to extreme poverty. The fate of such industries in the course of industrialization can thus have important impact on poverty during industrialization, and their role is not very different in modern industrializing countries than it was in the nineteenth century.

Why do we find the most vulnerable groups – the old, women, and children – employed in domestic industries? Low-strength requirements of most domestic tasks and easy access offer two explanations. In addition, domestic workers could, to a large degree, arrange the demands on their labor to accommodate supply, the latter determined by child rearing and outside labor demands. Working in domestic industries was especially convenient for women with children and for older people both because the work was located in the home and because the pace and timing of work was relatively flexible.

We have reasons to believe, therefore, that the presence of domestic or household industries and small land allotments reduced pauperism. They provided alternative income streams which became very important in the event of the chief wage earner being incapacitated, or of some collapse in the demand for market labor; they smoothed out the seasonal fluctuations in the demand for market labor; they provided employment for secondary workers in households headed by a primary worker; and they provided employment for those groups most vulnerable to poverty. While rarely agreeing on anything else, contemporary experts on poverty and the rural economy in late eighteenth-century England all agreed that the erosion of allotments and domestic industries in the south were a major cause of pauperism. Nor is this an attribute peculiar to England. In her study of pauperism in New York

State in the second quarter of the nineteenth century, Joan Hannon (1984, 1986) also found that household production was negatively correlated with pauperism.

Many studies have documented the effect of the demise of a particular household industry on employment opportunities for women and the elderly, and they always seem to be related to two key processes of economic development – market expansion and new technology. The story seems to be the same whether it is early nineteenth-century New England when the cotton textile factories wiped out domestic spinning almost overnight, or late eighteenth- and early nineteenth-century Ireland where factory competition from the Lancashire mills in England did the same. It would be a mistake, however, to give the impression that industrialization always displaces such secondary industries. It can also create them. A good historical example is offered by the evolution of technologies using cotton and wool. In the late eighteenth century, new factory-spinning technologies destroyed the household hand-spinning industry, but the cheaper thread it produced led to a boom in the household weaving industry. The number of handloom weavers in Britain increased by a factor of five between 1780 and 1810 to make use of the cheaper input that new factory-based technology had produced. In the early nineteenth century, new factory-weaving technologies then undercut the hand loom weavers so that by 1851 their number had returned to its 1780 level. Nor was this the end of the process. The new cheaper cloth was a factor in the emergence of new sweated clothes-making industries where it was an input. These industries also benefitted from technical changes such as the invention of the sewing machine. By the end of the century, however, even the sweated trades were being displaced by factory production.

The fact that the factory technologies which displaced one domestic industry often created another should not, however, lead us to the false conclusion that the extreme poor were unaffected on net. The new industries were often distant from those they replaced. And when an industry was overtaken by technology, the old were often in the worst position to adjust.

They lost a return on acquired, product-specific skills, and it was often hardest for them to migrate. A typical pattern appears to have been for the children of displaced workers to migrate while the old stayed put, suffering the falling wages and pauperism that accompanied deskilling.

How did industrialization affect seasonal fluctuations in labor demand? This is an important question since we know that seasonality in labor demand also produced seasonality in pauperism, especially among able bodied men. We have already noted that secondary industries tended to smooth the seasonal demand for labor either by having different peaks or by its inherent flexibility in time demands. The factory-induced destruction of the cottage industry was one reason why seasonal income cycles became more pronounced in eighteenth-century England. Increased crop specialization, driven by rising grain prices, had the same effect. This process also applied to America where western agriculture became increasingly linked to world markets by transport development, encouraging specialization in grain. Even as late as the 1890s farm laborers in Michigan were laid off 2.5 months per year, and the figure was 3.1 months among the unskilled in the building trades (Hatton and Williamson, 1990).

While these forces probably made the rural poor more vulnerable to seasonal rhythms in agriculture, they are not typical of the effect of development on seasonality. Even within agriculture new crops such as turnips spread out labor demands over the year. And although many industrial activities like construction remained seasonal, as development moved employment away from agriculture, it eventually led to a reduction in the importance of seasonal fluctuations in labor demand. This was clearly the main force at work. Indeed, MacKinnon (1986, p. 325) shows that the difference between summer and winter pauper rates declined across late nineteenth-century England.

While development may have reduced the problem of seasonality in labor demand, it increased the problem of market-oriented macro-shocks. To see the importance of macroeconomic cycles on poverty, figure 4.4 plots male able-bodied indoor pauper rates in three areas of England against unemployment from 1850 to 1910. (The short-run instability is due to the seasonal fluctuations discussed above). A strong relation between the pauper rates and unemployment is apparent, with pauperism following unemployment with a slight lag. This result is confirmed by regression analysis, as is the relationship between pauperism and other macroeconomic indicators (MacKinnon, 1984, 1986). The relationship between pauperism and the macroeconomy was strongest in the north where industrialization had proceeded furthest. Hannon argues that the changing structure of pauperism in the USA in the first half of the nineteenth century was also due to greater reliance on the market. Short-term unemployment became a more important cause of distress as households became more dependent on specialized wage labor and as domestic employment declined.

In short, poverty became more subject to market fluctuations in the late nineteenth century as technology, market development, and the division of labor led economic agents to be more closely dependent on the market and secondary activities were undermined. These secondary activities had been important supplements to primary household incomes especially during seasonal episodes of slack labor demand, and when macroeconomic shocks caused unemployment. They were also important as primary income sources for certain social groups from whom pauperization was a greater risk. One lesson we can take away from the nineteenth century is that it was the elderly and women with children who found it hardest to adapt to economic events which diminished access to secondary employment.

3 The Response of Policy to Poverty

A single issue will hold our attention for the remainder of this lecture and the book: the response of policy to poverty. We consider only two responses, although they were the most

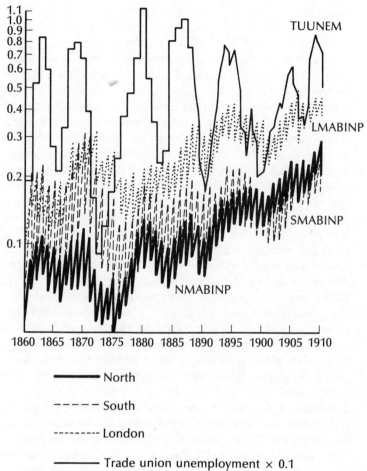

Figure 4.4 *Unemployment and male able-bodied indoor pauperism.*
Source: Mackinnon (1984, p. 299)

important two in the nineteenth century; social overhead investment in the cities and safety nets.

Social Overhead in the Cities

I showed in Lecture One that urban rents rose dramatically across the industrial revolution and that this had an especially damaging effect on the urban poor by raising their living costs. They made an effort to economize on the more expensive housing by crowding into very densely packed districts. At the same time, municipal authorities and planners found it extremely difficult to cope with the pollution and disamenities generated by the crowding in these rapidly growing cities. Thus, the cities became serious health hazards, so much so that Frederick Engels called them "killers." In contrast, today's cities in the Third World are relatively benign since, if anything, mortality rates are higher in the countryside. Not so in the nineteenth century, as table 4.4 shows for England (and things were no different on the Continent or in America). The death and sickness associated with this ugly environment fell most heavily, of course, on the poor and the extreme poor, those worst equipped to escape the environment. Sickness, mortality, and poverty are, of course, highly correlated, but how much of this result was simply due to a fact of policy, namely to underinvest in the social overhead of the cities?

Let me begin with what may appear to be an extraneous observation, although I think it is central to the story. As I argued in Lecture Three, Britain recorded very modest investment shares in national income by the standards of the contemporary Third World and the late nineteenth century. That fact has generated a long and active debate centered around the question: was the investment share low because investment requirements were modest, or was the investment share low because of a savings constraint? The first argues that investment demand in the private sector was the critical force driving accumulation during Britain's industrial revolution, low rates of technical progress and an absence of a capital-using bias both serving to minimize private-sector investment requirements. The second argues that Britain's growth was savings-constrained. Until very recently, the first view has dominated the literature.

One of the key reasons why *total* investment requirements during the First Industrial Revolution were so modest is that Britain failed to commit resources to those urban investment activities which make industrialization such a costly venture today, and which, in W. Arthur Lewis's (1978, p. 29) words, make contemporary Third World cities so capital-intensive.

Table 4.4 Infant Mortality Rates in England's Cities and Countryside, 1841, 1871, and 1906 (deaths per 1,000)

Region	1906	1871	1841
North			
Benign Countryside	145.3	156.1	114.8
Ugly Cities	148.8	212.1	174.5
Difference	+3.5	+56.0	+59.7
York			
Benign Countryside	138.9	163.5	138.3
Ugly Cities	149.5	189.4	171.7
Difference	+10.6	+25.9	+33.4
Lancs-Cheshire			
Benign Countryside	143.4	172.3	154.7
Ugly Cities	164.1	195.6	198.2
Difference	+20.7	+23.3	+43.5
Midlands			
Benign Countryside	116.8	124.9	137.0
Ugly Cities	145.4	193.2	190.2
Difference	+28.6	+68.3	+53.2
East and South			
Benign Countryside	110.5	154.3	129.8
Ugly Cities	133.0	170.9	173.2
Difference	+22.5	+16.6	+43.3

Source: Williamson (1990, Table 9.3)

Investment in housing and public works simply failed to keep pace with the rest of Britain's economy in the first half of the nineteenth century. While the total ACOR fell precipitously between 1800 and 1860, the ACOR for the total economy less agriculture, housing and public works actually *rose* over the same period. While the ACOR outside agriculture fell, implying modest investment requirements at the margin, the reason for it was that capital-intensive housing and public works were given short shrift.

Another way of illustrating this point is to examine the behavior of capital stock growth in social overhead – residential housing plus public works. Elsewhere (Williamson, 1990, ch. 10), I have shown that the stock of social overhead per capita fell in the late eighteenth century, contributing to a deterioration in the quality of life for the poor. This growth strategy continued for the first three decades of the nineteenth century, although not with quite the same intensity. Per capita stocks in public works continued to decline, but dwelling stocks per capita began to rise. The latter did not rise enough, however, to regain the levels of 1760. By 1830, therefore, Britain had accumulated an enormous deficit in her social overhead stocks by pursuing 70 years of industrialization on the cheap. It cost her dearly, as the social reformers were to point out.

All of this suggests that while actual investment requirements may have been modest during the First Industrial Revolution, they would *not* have been so modest had investment in social overhead kept pace. In contrast, consider twentieth-century industrial revolutions. W. Arthur Lewis spoke to this issue when he said: "The difference between the cost of urban and rural development does not turn on comparing the capital required for factories and that required for farms . . . The difference turns on infrastructure (Lewis, 1978, p. 29)." Indeed, when social overhead (including dwellings) is added to direct capital requirements, the capital–labor ratio in India's cities is about 4.5 times that of her rural areas (Becker, Williamson, and Mills, forthcoming, Table 3.1). In sharp contrast, when social overhead is included, Britain's cities look no more capital-intensive compared with the countryside than when the social overhead is excluded. While urban capital–labor ratios are about 4.5 times rural in India, they were about the same or less in mid nineteenth-century Britain. Cities are very capital-intensive in the contemporary Third World. Cities were relatively labor-intensive during the First Industrial Revolution. The difference appears to be explained in large part by a remarkably weak commitment to city social overhead in Britain.

City social overhead was low during the First Industrial Revolution. It lowered investment requirements, but it had its price since the cities became ugly, crowded and polluted, breeding high mortality and morbidity especially among the poor. In sharp contrast with the contemporary Third World, and to repeat, Britain's cities were killers: in 1841, city mortality rates were 5.6 per thousand *higher* than in the countryside; in 1960, Third World cities had mortality rates that were 6.3 per thousand *lower* than the countryside. We simply do not know how much of this stark demographic contrast between 1841 Britain and the contemporary Third World is due to Britain's low investment in city social overhead. Nor are we certain what contribution low investment in city social overhead made to the observed lag of life expectancy behind GNP gains (Fogel, 1986). But surely it mattered.

Evidence such as this invites the inference that more and earlier investment in city social overhead would have lowered mortality and morbidity, while raising the quality of life. But what would it have cost? Would it have been a good thing? Was *low* investment in city social overhead necessarily evidence of *underinvestment?* If Britain really did underinvest in city social overhead, then it should be manifested by high social rates of return to such investment. Reformists of that time certainly made the case that the cities were crowded and filthy, and that sickness and death were highly correlated with city ugliness, but to clinch the case for public intervention the reformers had to show clearly that public health investment would yield favorable returns.

So, what was the social rate of return to investment in

public health and cleaning up the cities? More than a decade ago, Edward Meeker (1974) used conventional benefit/cost analysis to estimate the social rate of return to investment in public health in American cities between 1880 and 1910, getting a range between 6 percent and 16 percent. Both of these social rates of return exceed private market rates at that time, and Meeker concluded that investment in public health and city social overhead was sound. It also implies, of course, that there was gross underinvestment in these activities even late in the century. It seems likely that it was even higher early in the century in Britain's cities. But if the social rate of return on investment in city social overhead was so high in the 1830s and 1840s, why was the level of investment so low? The explanation lies with failure of two kinds – capital-market failure and public-sector failure (Wohl, 1983; Williamson, 1990, ch. 10).

Safety Nets, the Family, and the State

Safety nets obviously matter to the poor. By safety nets, I mean those resources provided by the family, the community, or the state that support individuals during times of economic crisis. Without these safety nets, fluctuations in the incomes of the poor (or in their consumption capacity) will lead to high mortality and social disruption.

There is a commonly held myth about the historical evolution of safety nets. The myth has two parts. First, and during early stages of modern economic growth, industrialization and the emergence of markets both undermine a traditional agrarian society wherein the poor, the sick, and the old were all supported by extended families and the local village community. That is, in the traditional society the state played no active role. Second, and late in the industrialization process, formal institutions like social security are invented by modern governments which (finally) replace the traditional functions of family and charity in caring for the poor. In between these two stages lies an intermediate phase of development in which the dependence "on the market increases sharply (given the breakdown of the traditional peasant economy) and in which guaranteed entitlements in the form of social security benefits have yet to emerge" (Sen, 1977, p. 56).

Support for the second stage of this mythical evolution of safety nets is provided by Lindert's (1989) recent analysis of state-induced post-fisc redistributions, the key examples being the rise of twentieth-century welfare programs in Europe and North America. Certainly Lindert is correct in pointing out an increase in state support of the poor during the first two-thirds of this century. But this is only half the story. If we accept the myth of a simple two-stage path from "traditional" to "modern" safety nets, we will miss a key lesson of history.

The first big error embedded in the myth is its romanticized image of traditional society. The considerable efforts of demographic historians over the past three decades has made it clear that extended family systems were *never* the norm in north-western Europe (Hajnal, 1982), where, after all, the industrial revolution began. Far from undermining the extended family, industrialization may actually have strengthened it. Michael Anderson's (1972) studies of nineteenth-century Lancashire found more old people living with their married children in industrial Preston than in nearby rural areas. The same has been found in industrializing Massachusetts in the nineteenth century. Other studies of household structure may not provide a clear verdict on whether the extended family increased or decreased during the nineteenth century, but they *do* make it clear that the family was *not* the typical safety net in pre-industrial Britain. Such a finding is hardly surprising. Most parents did not live long enough to be a burden on their children anyway. As mortality rates fell during the industrial revolution, parents lived longer, giving them a greater opportunity to be supported by their children in old age. And their children, enjoying higher incomes, were better equipped to support them. On the other hand, children could better escape those responsibilities and default on their parents' investment in them by migrating to labor markets in distant towns at home or abroad.

There was, however, a safety net in pre-industrial Britain

and America that was threatened by nineteenth-century industrialization in both countries, and it was provided by – much to the surprise, I suspect, of many readers who have been victims of the myth – the *state*. From the seventeenth to the nineteenth century, "the collectivity rather than the family was the source of security for the individual over the life course" (Laslett, 1985, p. 360). The text of the famous Elizabethan Poor Law Act of 1601 explicitly confirms the responsibility of the state to support the same kind of individuals that were being supported by poor relief in the late nineteenth century: the old, the disabled, widows, orphans, and large families (Smith, 1981, p. 607). Evidence from four English communities suggests that one out of every five households were on some kind of relief in the eighteenth century (Smith, 1984, pp. 444–6), and that the generosity of state old-age pensions, relative to the market wage of the working poor, were in 1834 twice what they were in 1984 and even before Thatcher (Thomson, 1984, pp. 452–3). New York State relief programs at the start of the nineteenth century, and just prior to the industrial revolution, were as large a share of the state budget as federal welfare programs are in the US budget today (Hannon, 1986, pp. 1–3). So much for the myth that state welfare programs are an invention of modern governments. And so much for the myth that the industrial revolution displaced traditional family safety nets.

The existence of pre-industrial state support systems is explained in part by the absence of extended family networks. Nuclear family systems bring with them nuclear family risks. Formal state relief systems were a means of spreading those risks. But not all the poverty relieved by state intervention in pre-industrial England was attributable to the life cycle of nuclear families. Nor was the intervention solely restricted to poor relief. Robert Fogel (1989) has shown that food price intervention was regularly used by the early modern state in England to prevent famine. Like Amartya Sen's work on India, Fogel shifted our attention away from food shortage and towards low price elasticity of food demand. In local grain markets only poorly linked to national markets, prices rose sharply to eliminate excess demand, and in the absence of relief, poor net consumers of food could be forced into starvation. Price intervention muted local famines in pre-industrial England. And later, when food prices soared during the Napoleonic war, the Speenhamland system was created to supplement wages of the poor.

This sympathetic attitude towards poverty and generous safety nets for the poor did not persist after the Napoleonic wars when the industrial revolution gathered steam. And we see roughly the same swing in attitude and policy in the United States.

The most recurrent argument against poor relief on both sides of the Atlantic was that the poor were to blame for their fate, and that charity and relief merely removed the will to work. These arguments were not new even then. The same debates about who were and who were not the "deserving poor" are to be found in medieval writing. The difference is that this time these hostile views toward the poor did not go unanswered. Many who in the early nineteenth century opposed the generosity of poor relief or who called for a more stringent "workhouse test" were hardly very subtle in expressing their hostility. The most important proponent of tighter rules in the early nineteenth century was Malthus himself. Malthus agreed that society had ·an obligation to support the most needy, especially the old, but he believed that by supporting large families, poor relief encouraged popu-lation growth and thus depressed wages. A similar argument has recently resurfaced about English and American nine-teenth-century poor laws (Boyer, 1990; Hannon, 1986). In its modern guise, labor migration takes the place of fertility and mortality, and implicit contract theory takes the place of Malthusian demographics. But the story is familiar. By offer-ing poor relief to seasonally and cyclically idle farm laborers, out-migration was reduced and labor was made locally avail-able for the seasonal and cyclical peaks. Without such poor relief, employers who needed labor at times of peak demand would have had to offer higher wages and long-term contracts. Boyer and Hannon argue that early nineteenth-century poor relief in Britain and America was a way for employers to shift part of the cost of their implicit contracts with their workers onto the state.

Two other arguments used against generous poor relief should be familiar to those who follow contemporary debates over welfare reform. Opponents of outrelief were constantly worried that relief reduced incentives to work and save. Victorian opponents of poor relief also argued that it was socially damaging in that it undercut family and charitable responsibility. Nineteenth-century writers believed the myth that the family supplied support for the needy in the pre-industrial age. By cutting poor relief, they thought the mythical golden age would resurrect itself. Furthermore, the myth that state benefits were a recent substitute for extended family support and private charity helped to support the myth that formal benefits were not a "traditional" expectation.

The main swings in attitudes towards poor relief and poverty during the industrial revolution were as follows. In response to heightened seasonal unemployment (in the wake of enclosure and crop mix changes) and to high food prices (in the wake of the Napoleonic wars), poor relief became more generous by the end of the eighteenth century. The first part of the nineteenth century saw the emergence of an increasing concern about outrelief to the able-bodied as well as the generosity of that relief. The debate became heated on both sides of the Atlantic. It culminated with the passage in 1824 of a tougher New York State poor law and by a tougher new poor law in England in 1834. Both laws aimed to restrict outdoor relief. In the 1870s, again on both sides of the Atlantic, there was a so-called crusade against outrelief. During this period, outrelief was cut for many disadvantaged groups including widows and the elderly. Late in the century, we see some loosening up and an increased interest by social reformers in the poor, the most famous of which being Booth and Rowntree. While both attributed a great deal of poverty to the actions of the poor, they found much more "innocent" poverty than others had believed existed.

The 1900s are often seen as laying the foundation of modern welfarism. By 1914, England had old age pensions, some public "make-work" schemes, and less harsh attitudes towards the poor. This liberal surge around World War One ushered in what Lindert identifies as a widespread shift in attitudes among the NICs of that time, that is, the rise of redistributive schemes that had a significant impact on post-fisc income distributions. We should not forget, however, that the rise of the twentieth century welfare state represents a return to the more liberal attitudes towards the poor in pre-industrial Europe and America. It was only during the interim that nineteenth-century industrializing nations retreated from those liberal attitudes.

What was the effect of the less generous relief in Victorian England? For much of the poor, it is hard to say. We can be fairly sure, however, that the old were made much worse off. Figure 4.5 shows old-age pensions as a percentage of working-class adult incomes (Thomson, 1984, p. 453). The sharp decline in old-age support in the 1870s was large enough to imply an absolute fall in the income of the elderly. Indeed, there was a marked increase in the proportion of those over 65 in the workhouse during the 1870s and a similar increase in the ratio of inside to total non-able-bodied paupers (a group that includes the old) in the same period. MacKinnon (1984), p. 328) calculates that had there been no crusade against outrelief, there would have been 200,000 more old people given some outrelief in 1900, and the average working-class old person's income would have been 8 percent higher. While policy had a powerful negative impact on the elderly poor in the 1870s, it had an equally powerful positive impact in the early twentieth century. Following the introduction of old-age pensions in 1911, by 1913 outdoor pauperism among the elderly had fallen to 5 percent of its 1906 level.

What have we learned about safety nets? While it may be convenient to think otherwise, typically the poor in pre-industrial European and North American societies were *not* supported by the family and private institutions. In most leading nineteenth-century industrializers, a large part of the responsibility lay with the state and other formal, state-like

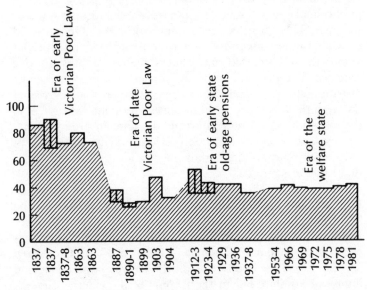

Figure 4.5 Pensions and working-class incomes: England, 1837–1981.
Source: Thomson (1984, p. 453)

institutions. These bodies intervened in food markets and their interventions mattered to the living standards of the poor. Where laissez-faire policies were adopted during the industrial revolution, as in America and England, many of the poor were big losers. The removal of traditional pre-industrial safety nets by laissez-faire-driven nineteenth-century industrial revolutions was viewed by many as the theft of what had come to be seen as a property right. We do not yet know by how much this "theft" hurt the poor, but it clearly mattered to those in extreme poverty at the bottom of the income distribution.

Epilogue

Does industrialization breed inequality? Does it increase poverty? Do either events foster accumulation? These were among the big questions in development economics prior to oil price shocks and the debt crisis, and they have always been among the big topics in economic history. With the appearance of rising inequality within the industrial nations in the 1980s, it has become a fashionable topic once again even there. Oddly enough, the contemporary debate in the Third World, and more recently in industrial nations, has not been well informed by history. This book, based on the Yale Kuznets lectures, tries to redress that balance. Indeed, Simon Kuznets himself devoted a good share of his prolific scholarly output to the same goal.

To be quite frank, the evidence on each of these three variables is sufficiently flawed to ensure that the debate over what really happens during industrial revolutions is likely to continue for some time. But there is enough historical evidence to suggest that: most newly industrializing countries in the 19th century did undergo rising inequality before undergoing rising equality in the 20th century; most did not undergo a rise in poverty rates, although the rate of escape from poverty was slow where rising inequality was pronounced; rising inequality never played a critical role in making rising rates of non-human capital accumulation possible; and rising inequality did play a critical role in making rising rates of human capital accumulation difficult. These are four important historical morals. While the evidence carrying these morals can and has been criticized, it is persuasive enough to warrant more serious thinking about what accounts for these events when they appear, as well as about what accounts for their absence when they do not.

I hope this book will help stimulate further thinking along these lines. I also hope it will encourage participants in the debate to take a closer look at history. If the book fails to persuade, but succeeds to provoke, then I will be content.

References

Adelman, I. and C. T. Morris (1978), "Growth and Impoverishment in the Middle of the Nineteenth Century," *World Development* 6 (3), pp. 245–73.

Ahluwalia, M. S. (1976), "Inequality, Poverty and Development," *Journal of Development Economics* 3 (4), pp. 307–42.

—— (1980), "Growth and Poverty in Developing Countries," in H. Chenery (ed.), *Structural Change and Development Policy* (New York: Oxford University Press).

Anderson, M. (1972), "Household Structure and the Industrial Revolution: Mid 19th Century Preston in Comparative Perspective," in P. Laslett (ed.), *Household and Family in Past Time* (Cambridge: Cambridge University Press).

Ashton, T. S. (1955), *An Economic History of England: The 18th Century* (London: Methuen).

—— (1959), *Economic Fluctuations in England, 1700–1800* (Oxford: Clarendon Press).

Bacha, E. L. (1979), "The Kuznets Curve and Beyond: Growth and Change in Inequalities," in E. Malinvaud (ed.), *Economic Growth and Resources, Vol. 1, Major Issues* (New York: St Martins).

Becker, C. M., J. G. Williamson, and E. S. Mills (forthcoming), *Indian Urbanization and Economic Growth Since 1960* (Baltimore, Md: Johns Hopkins University Press).

Blinder, A. S. (1980), "The Level and Distribution of Economic Well-Being," in M. Feldstein (ed.), *The American Economy in Transition* (Chicago: University of Chicago Press).

Bowley, A. L. and A. R. Burnett-Hurst (1915), *Livelihood and Poverty* (London: Ratan Tata Foundation, Bell and Sons).

Bowley, A. L. and M. Hogg (1925), *Has Poverty Diminished?* (London: King and Son).

Boyer, G. B. (1990) *An Economic History of the English Poor Law, 1750–1850* (Cambridge: Cambridge University Press).

Chenery, H., M. S. Ahluwalia, C. L. G. Bell, J. H. Duloy, and R. Jolly (1974), *Redistribution with Growth* (London: Oxford University Press).

Clark, C. (1957), *The Conditions of Economic Progress* (London: Macmillan, 3rd edn).

Cline, W. R. (1972), *Potential Effects of Income Redistribution on Economic Growth: Latin American Cases* (New York: Praeger).

Corden, M. and R. Findlay (1975), "Urban Unemployment Intersectoral Capital Mobility and Development Policy," *Economica* 42, pp. 59–78.

Deane, P. and W. A. Cole (1962), *British Economic Growth 1688–1959* (Cambridge: Cambridge University Press).

Denison, E. F. (1967), *Why Growth Rates Differ: Postwar Experience in Nine Western Countries* (Washington, DC: The Brookings Institution).

—— and W. K. Chung (1976), *How Japan's Economy Grew So Fast* (Washington, DC: The Brookings Institution).

Dougherty, C. and M. Selowsky (1973), "Measuring the Effects of the Misallocation of Labor," *Review of Economics and Statistics* 55, pp. 386–90.

Easterlin, R. A. (1981), "Why Isn't the Whole World Developed?," *Journal of Economic History* 41 (1), pp. 1–19.

Edelstein, M. (1982), *Overseas Investment in the Age of High Imperialism: The United Kingdom, 1850–1914* (New York: Columbia University Press).

Fei, J. C. H. and G. Ranis (1964), *Development of a Labor Surplus Economy: Theory and Policy* (Homeword, Ill.: Irwin).

Feinstein, C. (1988), "The Rise and Fall of the Williamson Curve," *Journal of Economic History* 48, pp. 699–729.

Fields, G. S. (1989), "Poverty, Inequality, and Economic

Growth," World Bank Working Paper (Washington, DC).

Fogel, R. W. (1986), "Nutrition and the Decline in Mortality Since 1700: Some Preliminary Findings," in S. L. Engerman and R. E. Gallman (eds), *Longterm Factors in American Economic Growth*, NBER Studies in Income and Wealth, vol. 51 (Chicago: Chicago University Press).

—— (1989), "Second Thoughts on the European Escape from Hunger: Famine, Price Elasticities, Entitlements, Chronic Malnutrition, and Mortality Rates," NBER/DAE Working Paper No. 1 (Cambridge, Mass.: National Bureau of Economic Research, May).

Ford, P. and G. Ford (1969), *A Breviate of British Parliamentary Papers 1900–16* (Shannon, Ireland: Irish University Press).

Hagen, E. E. (1958), "An Economic Justification of Protection," *Quarterly Journal of Economics* 72, pp. 496–514.

Hajnal, J. (1982), "Two Kinds of Preindustrial Household Formation Systems," *Population and Development Review*, 8 (3).

Hannon, J. U. (1984), "Poverty and the Antebellum Northeast: The View from New York State's Relief Rolls," *Journal of Economic History* 44, pp. 1,007–32.

—— (1986), "Dollars, Morals, and Markets: The Shaping of Nineteenth Century Poor Relief Policy," paper prepared for the University of California Intercampus Group in Economic History Conference on *Searching for Security: Poverty, Old Age, and Dependency in the Nineteenth Century*.

Hatton, T. J. and J. G. Williamson (1989), "What Explains Wage Gaps Between Farm and City? Exploring the Todaro Model with American Evidence 1890–1941," HIER Discussion Paper No. 1433, Harvard University (April).

—— (1990), "Unemployment, Implicit Contracts, and Compensating Wage Differentials: Michigan in the 1890s," Department of Economics, Harvard University (February).

Hoselitz, B. F. (1957), "Urbanization and Economic Growth in Asia," *Economic Development and Cultural Change* 5, pp. 42–54.

Kelley, A. C. and J. G. Williamson (1984), *What Drives Third World City Growth?* (Princeton: Princeton University Press).

Kuznets, S. (1955), "Economic Growth and Income Inequality," *American Economic Review* 45 (1), pp. 1–28.

—— (1976), "Demographic Aspects of the Size Distribution of Income: An Exploratory Essay, *Economic Development and Cultural Change* 25 (1), pp. 1–94.

Laslett, P. (1985), "Gregory King, Robert Malthus, and the Origins of English Social Realism," *Population Studies* 39 (3), pp. 351–63.

Leibenstein, H. (1957), "The Theory of Underemployment in Backward Economies," *Journal of Political Economy* 65, pp. 91–103.

Lewis, W. A. (1954), "Economic Development with Unlimited Supplies of Labour," *Manchester School of Economic and Social Studies* 22, pp. 139–91.

—— (1965), "A Review of Development Theory," *American Economic Review* 55, pp. 1–16.

—— (1978), *The Evolution of the International Economic Order* (Princeton, NJ: Princeton University Press).

Lindert, P. H. (1986), "Unequal English Wealth Since 1670," *Journal of Political Economy* 94, pp. 1,127–62.

—— (1989), "Modern Fiscal Redistribution: A Preliminary Essay," Department of Economics, University of California, Davis (May).

Lindert, P. H. and J. G. Williamson (1985), "Growth, Equality, and History," *Explorations in Economic History* 22 (4), pp. 341–77.

Lipton, M. (1976), *Why Poor People Stay Poor: Urban Bias in World Development* (Cambridge, Mass.: Harvard University Press).

MacFarlane, A. (1978), *The Origins of English Individualism* (London: Oxford University Press).

Mackinnon, Mary (1984), *Poverty and Policy: The English Poor Law 1860–1910*, unpublished D.Phil. thesis, University of Oxford.

—— (1986), "Poor Law Policy, Unemployment, and Pauperism," *Explorations in Economic History* 23, pp. 299–336.

Margo, R. A. and G. C. Villaflor (1987), "The Growth of

Wages in Antebellum America: New Evidence," *Journal of Economic History* 47, pp. 873–95.

Mathias, P. (1972), "Preface" in F. Crouzet (ed.), *Capital Formation in the Industrial Revolution* (London: Methuen).

Meeker, E. (1974), "The Social Rate of Return on Investment in Public Health, 1880–1910," *Journal of Economic History* 34 (2), pp. 392–421.

Morley, S. A. (1981), "The Effect of Changes in the Population on Several Measures of Income Distribution," *American Economic Review* 71 (3), pp. 285–94.

Morris, C. T. and I. Adelman (1988), *Comparative Patterns of Economic Development 1850–1914* (Baltimore: Johns Hopkins University Press).

Musgrove, P. (1980), "Income Distribution and the Aggregate Consumption Function," *Journal of Political Economy* 88, pp. 504–25.

Neal, L. (1985), "Integration of International Capital Markets: Quantitative Evidence from the Eighteenth to Twentieth Centuries," *Journal of Economic History* 45, pp. 219–26.

Paukert, F. (1973), "Income Distribution at Different Levels of Development: A Survey of Evidence," *International Labour Review* 108 (2–3), pp. 97–125.

Polak, B. and J. G. Williamson (1989), "Poverty, Policy, and Industrialization: Lessons from the Distant Past," background paper for the *World Development Report 1990* (Washington, DC: IBRD, September).

Preston, S. H. (1985), "The Changing Relation Between Mortality and Level of Economic Development," *Population Studies* 29 (2), pp. 231–48.

Preston, S. H. and E. van de Walle (1978), "Urban French Mortality in the Nineteenth Century," *Population Studies* 32 (2), pp. 275–97.

Riley, J. C. (1987), *The Eighteenth Century Campaign to Avoid Disease* (London: Macmillan).

Robinson, S. (1976), "A Note on the U Hypothesis Relating Income Inequality and Economic Development," *American Economic Review* 66 (3), pp. 437–40.

Rowntree, B. S. (1901, new edn 1908), *Poverty: A Study of Town Life* (London: MacMillan).

Schultz, T. P. (1987), "School Expenditures and Enrollments, 1960–1980: The Effects of Income, Prices, and Population Growth," in D. G. Johnson and R. D. Lee (eds), *Population Growth and Economic Development: Issues and Evidence* (Madison, Wisconsin: University of Wisconsin Press).

Scott, J. C. (1976), *The Moral Economy of the Peasant* (New Haven: Yale).

Sen, A. K. (1977), "Famines, Food Availability, and Exchange Entitlements," *Cambridge Journal of Economics* 1, pp. 33–59.

—— (1981), *Poverty and Famines* (London: Oxford University Press).

Smith, J. E. (1984), "Widowhood and Aging in Traditional English Society," *Aging and Society* 4 (4), pp. 429–49.

Smith, R. E. (1981), "Fertility, Economy, and Household Formation in England," *Population and Development Review* 7 (4), pp. 595–622.

Squire, L. (1981), *Employment Policy in Developing Countries* (Oxford: Oxford University Press).

Thompson, E. P. (1971), "The Moral Economy of the English Crowd in the 18th Century," *Past and Present* 50, pp. 76–136.

Thomson, D. (1984), "The Decline of Social Welfare: Falling State Support for the Elderly Since Early Victorian Times," *Ageing and Society* 4 (4), pp. 451–82.

Tinbergen, J. (1975), *Income Distribution: Analysis and Policies* (Amsterdam: North Holland).

Todaro, M. P. (1969), "A Model of Labor Migration and Urban Unemployment in Less Developed Countries," *American Economic Review* 59 (1), pp. 138–48.

Williams, Karel (1981), *From Pauperism to Poverty* (London: Routledge & Kegan Paul).

Williamson, J. G. (1979), "Inequality, Accumulation, and Technological Imbalance: A Growth–Equity Conflict in American History?," *Economic Development and Cultural Change* 27 (2), pp. 231–53.

—— (1984), "Why Was British Growth So Slow During the

Industrial Revolution?," *Journal of Economic History* 44 (3), pp. 687–712.

—— (1985a), *Did British Capitalism Breed Inequality?* (Boston: Allen & Unwin).

—— (1985b), "The Historical Content of the Classical Labor Surplus Model," *Population and Development Review* 11 (2), pp. 171–91.

—— (1986a), "Did Rising Emigration Cause Fertility to Decline in 19th Century Rural England? Child Costs, Old-Age Pensions, and Child Default," paper presented to the *Tenth Conference of the University of California Intercampus Group in Economic History*, Laguna Beach, Ca. (May 2–4).

—— (1986b), "The Impact of the Corn Laws Just Prior to Repeal," HIER Discussion Paper No. 1279, Harvard University (November).

—— (1987), "Did English Factor Markets Fail During the Industrial Revolution?," *Oxford Economic Papers* 39, pp. 641–8.

—— (1989a), "Inequality and Modern Economic Growth: What Does History Tell Us?" *Kuznets Memorial Lectures*, Yale University, New Haven, Ct (September 20–22).

—— (1989b), "Human Capital Deepening, Inequality, and Demographic Events Along the Asian Pacific Rim," paper presented at the Conference on the *Sources of Economic Dynamism in the Asian and Pacific Region*, Nihon University, Tokyo (November 20–23).

—— (1990), *Coping with City Growth During the British Industrial Revolution* (Cambridge: Cambridge University Press).

Williamson, J. G. and P. H. Lindert (1980), *American Inequality: A Macroeconomic History* (New York: Academic Press).

Wohl, A. S. (1983), *Endangered Lives: Public Health in Victorian Britain* (Cambridge: Cambridge University Press).

Zevin, R. B. (1989), "Are World Financial Markets More Open? If So, Why and With What Effects?", in *Financial Openness and National Autonomy* (New York: Oxford University Press).

Index